Seeds

The seed, the soil and me
Dawn Finch

I let the beautiful golden discs turn to wrinkled brown, then black, and waited for the seeds. ...

~ Dawn Finch, this volume

When I was nine years old, my dad gave me a packet of sunflower seeds. I planted them out in a small patch of dirt behind the shed. As spring turned to summer I cared for my little green babies. Taller and taller they grew until they towered over me. Neighbours commented over the low fences as my sunflowers stretched upwards, turning their faces to the sun with heads as large as dinner plates. That summer I was the talk of the neighbourhood as my sunflowers could be seen over the gardens, tossing their golden petals in the breeze. I was so proud.

I let the beautiful golden discs turn to wrinkled brown, then black, and waited for the seeds. When the time came, my dad cut the towering plants down for me and I left the heads dry out on my windowsill in the last rays of the year. Then I collected the seeds and laid them out to dry, and then filled a jar with them. That jar lived in the dark under my bed as a memento of the summer, and a reminder of the spring yet to come.

Spring came and I was so excited to get my little seeds into soil. I had my pots filled with compost and I set them up on the windowsill in the shed. This was where my disappointment began. I did exactly the same as I'd done before, but fewer than half of my seeds showed their little green noses above the soil and the ones that did were weak. The weeks rolled on and my sunflowers failed to thrive. They grew spindly and nothing I did made a difference. When they eventually flowered their blooms were no bigger than my hand and they waved their apologetically small faces at me as I peeped around the shed to check on them.

The crushing disappointment meant I didn't grow sunflowers again until adulthood. What I didn't realise then was that there was nothing I could have done to make those second-year sunflowers a success because I was a victim of the F1 hybrid seed trap. I didn't know that the seeds I had so carefully gathered and kept all winter were doomed to return to type and instead only grew a weak version of one of the original sunflowers used by the hybrid creators.

The F1 hybrid seed trap

Most of the seeds we now see available to us have been cross-bred to create seeds that are strong, reliable and in many cases resistant to disease. Cross-breeding plants for a better end result is nothing new. The desire for larger fruit, better colour, more vigorous habit has driven cross breeding for millennia. Growers want bigger, better plants which have a lower failure rate and that can come from these commercially produced seeds, but at a cost. F1 hybrid seed is basically a seed created by cross-breeding and the commercial seed creators want to protect their creation to protect their investment. Creating hybrid F1 seed is an expensive process and the seed producer has to maintain the original "pure" lines to create more of this stronger, faster, bigger seed. This means that the seed is more expensive, and because of the hybridisation process the plant you grow from it will not set viable seed that you can use in your own allotment or garden. Seed gathered from plants raised from F1 hybrid seed will grow a plant that will revert to one or other of the original parent plants. It will not grow the plant you had last year. After one season hybrid seed will revert to its true nature rather than the enhanced version you grew because it is not seed from a plant that has naturally adapted and evolved over many generations of growth. Hybrid seed is from a plant that has had this process forced upon it for a single season of growth and it is unable to reliably hold those qualities to further

3

seasons.

There is no doubt that there is a financial draw for commercial growers to use F1 hybrid seed, but there is another way. This is to seek out heirloom or open pollinated varieties. Open pollinated plants are those which are either self-pollinating or will cross with their neighbours, and heirloom varieties are open-pollinated plants that are over 50 years old. These are plants that are pollinated by wind or natural pollinators like insects. These plants are the ones that are most genetically variable and likely to adapt over generations to changing conditions and climates. These are the plants from which we can collect seed, and share seed, and grow on from generation to generation.

It is only two or three generations ago that almost all of our food came from open-pollinated varieties but, over the last 50 years, thousands of varieties have disappeared from the seeds lists. The science that dominates the agricommerce industry has focussed almost exclusively on creating F1 hybrid seed. The seed industry has, over this relatively short period of time, achieved an inbuilt dependence on them as growers purchase new seeds every year. It is, after all, a huge business and their income depends on growers re-buying their seeds every year.

For those of us interested in freeing ourselves from that self-perpetuating trap of repurchasing seeds every year, there is seed saving. Seed saving itself is a learned skill and there is something intrinsically beautiful about learning the many and varied methods of pollination of these varieties.

Seed

I hold the future in my palm
Bloom dried
past weathered to hard skin
that speaks in silent whisper
of soil
and sun
and rain
and of seasons chorused through by insect hum
After all our shared challenges
there is this tiny thing
In the circle of this journey
in this small hard casing
is all the Earth

Seed saving for beginners

Our starting place as seed savers is to always choose open-pollinated or heirloom varieties to grow. The next thing you should learn when growing for success is how your plants propagate. Your vegetables will reproduce either by cross pollination, self-pollination or a combination of both. Most will be insect pollinated, but some, including sweetcorn, spinach, chard and beetroot for example, are pollinated by wind. Try to learn the method of propagation for the plant you wish to grow and encourage this environment for the plant. For example, if your plant is propagated by insects and you are spraying everything with pesticides you will never collect seed from it. If it needs the wind and you've got it shut up in polytunnel, you won't have the results you need.

Growing for seed takes advance planning too. Once you have chosen which crop you wish to gather seed from, you should take particular care to maintain those plants long after you have harvested the other fruit or vegetables from that patch. It is also wise to make sure you are selecting the finest and healthiest looking plants to set seed. There is no point in collecting seed from the plants that were weak or that failed to thrive because there is every chance their seeds will do the same. It is wise to keep a seed diary so you can track growth for things like germination time and time between fruit, flower and seed. It is not simply a case of leaving things to "go over", but to shift your mindset to a place where you are looking at two crops from your plants; the crop you eat, and the crop you plan to grow next year.

Some plants are easier to save seed from than others, but a good place to start is to examine the crops we most commonly grow in our home plots.

Tomatoes

Tomatoes are self-pollinating plants and don't normally accidentally cross too readily with other cultivated varieties. The only exception to this is some very old varieties with flowers that have very pronounced stigmas. To get good seed from tomatoes it is wise to keep single varieties together, and a short distance apart from other tomato types you might be growing. Don't mix them up in the same bed or spaces, and aim to grow different varieties 50 cm to a metre apart from each other.

Good tomato seed depends on growing strong

and healthy plants. Feed them well with natural tomato feed such as a homemade comfrey tea and support the plants well as they grow. [1] Unsupported plants will have to put so much effort into their stems that it will waste energy it could be using to grow fruit. Your tomato plants need plenty of airflow and lots of insect visits. Like many plants the caress of the breeze and the attention of insects will release the pollen.

When you harvest for seed, make sure you only pick the fruits that are perfect examples of the type. Pick the healthiest and lushest tomatoes because they will be the manifestation of the seed within. Allow them to fully ripen on the bough, and then to go slightly over-ripe.

Tomato seed is collected wet and you should cut the fruit in half and gently remove the seeds and their gelatinous coating. Place the seeds in bowl and cover with water. Leave this mix at room temperature for 3–4 days. Over this time the mix

---

1. Comfrey tea is very easy to make. Fill a water-tight bucket or container full of comfrey leaves; use a brick or a stone to weigh down the leaves; leave for several weeks; collect the smelly liquid; dilute 1:10 with water to use as a liquid fertiliser. See also weed tea in *Compost* in this collection.

will develop a sort of scum on top as a fermentation process dissolves the gel around the seed. The seeds will sink to the bottom and the scum on the top can be skimmed off before the seeds are drained and rinsed clean.

Place the wet seeds on kitchen paper, pat dry, and place between two sheets of dry kitchen paper. The drying seeds should be kept in a warm and well aired place as you really need them to dry rapidly to avoid them germinating. When you are absolutely sure they are dry, store them well (somewhere dry and not too hot).

Peas

Peas are probably the seeds many people have saved first, in fact they are thought to be one of the earliest cultivated crops. Evidence has even been found of dried and stored peas from Neolithic sites. They are naturally self-pollinating and they don't really cross-pollinate easily, but it does make sense to just grow the type you like to eat. It's almost impossible to tell if your peas have cross-pollinated because they look so alike—literally like peas in a pod! They are definitely one of the easiest seeds to save, so easy I find it baffling that people buy them!

I've grown peas I've found in random bags in the shed, and I've even successfully grown peas from dried soup mix from the supermarket. Of course random peas will give you random plants and it is worth giving some thought to the peas you save to make your crops better.

Start your pea saving by thinking about the kind of peas you actually enjoy eating. When you have decided which peas you would like to grow, it is worth sowing them in 3 or 4 times the number you feel you'll need. You can thin the weedy ones down and eat the shoots in a salad, so nothing is wasted.

In an ideal year of long summer weather with friendly breezes and good occasional rain, you should leave your peas to mature on the vine. Let them turn brown and get to the point where the peas are rattling in their dry cases. If you live in a zone where the autumn leaps upon you with soggy boots, you can dry the pods indoors or in a greenhouse. Cut the whole plant and hang it upside down to let the very last nutrients pour into the pods. You'll need good airflow to make sure that the pods do not mould, and do discard any that look as if they are getting furry. It can take weeks to dry out peas properly and you should resist temptation to put your peas into storage until you are completely sure they are dry. Don't be tempted to put them in a dehydrator or oven because this will be too rapid a drying process and the seed will be baked rather than gently falling into a dormant state.

Store your peas in a sterile and airtight jar and make sure you label it clearly with the variety and any notes. If you put a tablespoon of uncooked rice in the bottom of the jar it will help draw out any last traces of moisture. They should keep for a couple of years in dark place.

Beans

Beans are pretty friendly plants and they will cross with other beans that you are growing close by. This means that if you really want to protect the type you are growing (for example if you are growing an heirloom variety) you should grow just one type or keep them a good distance from each other. Commercial growers say you should aim for around 20 metres between varieties, but obviously that's not possible for most of us! Bean pollen is transferred by your insect pollinators and these will bounce around your plants sharing the love. To protect the seed from an heirloom variety you can grow your beans in a large circular patch and harvest your seeds from the plants right in the middle of the patch. That way the pollinators will have bumbled around and deposited most of their pollen on the outside edge plants and you'll have a better chance of keeping your seed true to type.

At the end of the season let some good strong pods mature and dry on the plant and harvest as late as you can. Lay the pods dry and warm inside to mature for their final stage for at least two weeks, then you can take them out of their pods. Spread them out on clean, dry, teatowels or kitchen paper and let the beans dry out completely. Store in clean and sterile jars, but beans like a colder storage so you can wrap the jar well in newspaper and store it in your shed.

Beets and chard

Beetroot, spinach, Swiss chard, and leaf beet all come from the same family and they will happily cross with each other. As they are wind pollinated there really isn't much you can do about it as their pollen can carry for miles on the breeze. If we're not fussy about leaf beets and chards crossing, then we can leave them to get on with it! They are biennial plants and will flower in their second year and this means you should leave some strong plants to over-winter and then let them flower and go to seed the following year. The seed you gather will be genetically mixed, but if it's survived a full year of your climate then the seed from those plants is going to grow into some subtly adapted plants.

If you are absolutely dead-set on maintaining true to type seeds, you will have to isolate plants from which you wish to harvest seed. The simplest way to do this is to cover the flowers with a fine mesh bag, and give it a little shake from time to time to distribute the pollen inside the bag.

The seeds of beets and chards will be prickly and a bit like little cork balls. Beet and chard flowers bolt straight up from the parent plant with tightly packed clusters of tiny flowers. Watch the plant carefully as the flowers go to seed as they will drop seeds and you will lose them in the soil. Harvest them as they start to turn brown. You can cut the whole stem and rub the seedstalk gently to release the corky seed from the plant.

13

Carrots

Carrots are biennial too and, like beets, will flower in their second year. Identify your fattest and healthiest carrots (a little scraping back of soil will allow you a peep at them) and these will be your seed plants. Let the foliage die back at the end of the season and then cover them with a good layer of mulch or compost for the winter. If you live in an area of very harsh winters you should lift your carrots and store them in a box of dry sand. When the spring comes you can carefully replant the carrots and they will start to sprout again. These carrots will then want to flower and make seed. Carrots will grow tall plants when they are wanting to flower and are insect pollinated so it's very important that you are growing other plants to attract sufficient pollinators.

Carrot flowers form umbrella-like clusters of flowers known as umbels. Your carrots might form a number of umbels but you should save your seed from only the first and second of them as they will be the biggest. Keep the cut head somewhere warm and dry and to gather the seeds you can rub the heads between your hands. Carrot seeds are a bit fluffy and have what is known as a "beard" attached to them. You can spend ages rubbing the seed to make a tidier looking seed by removing the beard, but there really is no need. Nature has given the seed that beard to help it anchor in the soil rather than wash away in heavy rainfall. The reason commercial seed has the beard removed is because beardless seed goes through industrial sowing equipment easier. Personally, I think life is too short to de-beard carrot seeds!

In short …

A little research will give you advice specific to each and every plant in your patch, but there are a few tips common to all plants.

- Don't leave seed saving to the last minute, think in advance about the needs of your plants and make it happen right through its growing cycle

- Watch your plants carefully for the strongest and most true-to-type individuals and gather your seeds from them. The parent plant will give you an idea of what to expect from the

15

seed.

- Storage matters. Take care with your labelling and storage. Don't put all that effort into saving your seeds to then consign them to confusion and mould over winter

- Never forget your pollinators! There can be very few of us who are not aware of the vital role that insects play in our gardens. If you spray to remove or prevent the insects you don't want, you will inevitably be destroying the insects you *do* want. If you want successful seed it is far better to work with nature, than against it. Instead of spraying against aphids, grow companion plants that will encourage useful pollinators like hover flies and ladybirds to eat them. You won't produce successful seed without pollinators. I tend to work with the mindset that I'm growing a third for this year's table, a third for next year's, and a third for the wee beasties!

Alloted Time

In this place I linger
bone tired
sun warmed
muddied and with soil beneath my nails
and sun freckled across my skin
The day rolls on through its palette of blue
I linger here while Summer's tail flicks at Autumn's feet
and the changing seasons draw my plants to seed
A promise of years to come in their curled pods
and faded flowers
mouse nibbled
bee blessed
I breathe deep
and watch the light fade on the boughs
and pretend not to see shrews steal through the peas
and birds digging between the beets
Unwilling to leave
in this place I linger

Why bother saving seed?

Obviously, it will save you a lot of money to save your own seed, but there is also something deeply satisfying about being able to take your plants full cycle. To take a seed from one of your own plants and bring it all the way around to seed again is a beautiful thing. It is also a manifestation of the control we can take back from commercial hybrid seed suppliers. We haven't had to pay for the privilege of using sterile seed for one season, because this belongs to our land. We can know this plant. We can take that seed and know absolutely where it has come from. By raising or sharing our own seed we are also playing a surer hand because we know it survived in this climate, and this soil, and this environment the previous year, and the one before that. Growers can take their saved seeds and swap them with friends and together we can mix up the genetic pool and create seed that is uniquely suited to our parts of the world.

There is more to it than that though. For me there is something deeply personal in this cyclical process. The plant and I did this together in a symbiotic relationship. The plant fed me and in my gratitude I will do my best to help it to perpetuate its life cycle. Thanks to the journey we have taken together I have learnt the needs of this plant. I learnt how it lasted the wind, and the rain. I can tell if it will enjoy certain types of feed, and if it likes an open breezy spot, or a warm sheltered place. This plant and I went through this process together and that makes me feel a curious bond to the plants I bring to seed. At the end of the season, when I hold that seed, there is in my mind the knowledge that this is another beginning and the plant and I will see each other again. When it cracks its tiny shell and reaches those first green shoots up through the dark, damp soil seeking the sunlight, I will be there waiting patiently for it—again.

Further resources

Cherfas, Jeremy. *The Seed Savers' Handbook* (UK: Eco-logic Books, 1996).

Etty, Thomas and Harrison, Lorraine. *Heirloom Plants: A Complete Compendium of Heritage Vegetables, Fruit, Herbs and Flowers* (UK: Ivy Press, 2015).

Gorer, Richard (ed.). *Fruit and Vegetables from Seed: An Illustrated Dictionary* (UK: Magnolia, 1982).

Heistinger, Andrea. *The Manual of Seed Saving: Harvesting, Storing and Sowing Techniques* (USA: Timber Press, 2013).

Jeffrey, Josie. *Seedswap: The gardener's guide to saving and swapping seeds* (Boulder: Roost Books, 2014).

Phillips, Catherine. *Saving More Than Seed: Practices and Politics of Seed Saving* (New York: Routledge: 2016).

Silvertown, Jonathan. *An Orchard Invisible: A Natural History of Seeds* (Chicago: University of Chicago Press, 2009).

Stickland, Sue. *Back Garden Seed Saving: Keeping our vegetable heritage alive* (UK: Eco-logic Books:, 2008). We recommend this book as a good place to begin seed saving.

Online resources

DIY Seeds. https://www.diyseeds.org/en/films/ A lot of very useful videos!

Garden Organic. https://www.gardenorganic.org.uk/seed-saving-guidelines.

Organic Seed Alliance. https://seedalliance.org/publications/seed-saving-guide-gardeners-farmers.

Real Seeds. https://www.realseeds.co.uk/seed-savinginfo.html.

Seed Sovereignty. https://www.seedsovereignty.info/resources/seed-saving-resources.

Strathbogie Seed Collective. https://www.facebook.com/groups/1100807860258553.

Dawn Finch likes to regard herself as a child of the land and her ancestors were gamekeepers and farmers. She grew up in acres of landscaped rose gardens as her father was one of the UK's most respected rose experts, and her sister is a renowned floral artist. With her passion for fruit and vegetables, Dawn is affectionately regarded as the odd one out of the family!

Dawn is a curator of the Strathbogie Seed Collective seed library, and is also the cook and owner of Plot 9 Preserves and Neep&Okra. She is a bestselling author of non-fiction books for children and is a poet and twice winner of the Brian Nisbett Poetry Award.

Town is the Garden

A community food growing project, *of sorts*.

For three years the Town is the Garden team could be found at the margins of the garden. Amongst the weeds and compost heaps, they explored what it might mean to *think with* the garden. Through crafting gardens, vegetable plots and orchards they attempted to rethink how a community might feed itself as it faces up to the global climate and ecological emergency. Through the processes of learning and sharing skills in relation to growing food, from planting seeds to preserving the harvest, they asked how we might also begin to pay better attention to the entanglement of human and more-than-human worlds. They asked how might the garden be a site of both resistance and resilience? A place for *thinking* and *doing* ecology, otherwise.

This is *Seeds* in a collection of seven chapbooks by the *Town is the Garden* that attempt to capture some of the diverse ways of thinking, doing and knowing the project explored with some of the people they explored them with. It includes contributions from Eleanor Brown and Alexandra Falter (*Plants*), Jonathan Baxter & Sarah Gittins (*Orchard*), Joe Crowdy (*Garden*), Dawn Finch

(*Seeds*), Maria Puig de la Bellacasa (*Compost*), and Joss Allen, Caroline Gatt and Elisabetta Rattalino (*Story*). With cover illustrations by Jamie Johnson.

The Town is the Garden team included: Joss Allen (2017–20), Rhian Davies (2019–20), Caroline Gatt (2018–20), Camille Sineau (2017–18), and Lindy Young (2017–19).

https://www.deveron-projects.com/town-garden

The *Town is the Garden* team would like to thank everyone who contributed to these chapbooks and Footprint Workers Cooperative for their exceptional printing skills.

A massive thank you to everyone at Deveron Projects, staff, board and interns (too many to name), especially Petra Pennington, Robyn Wolsey and Claudia Zeiske—for their support and guidance—and the Neep & Okra Kitchen team—with whom we latterly shared space and ideas with. To Alex Severn, our wonderful intern, on a student placement from the University of Aberdeen. To our generous funders Aberdeenshire Council, Action Earth, Climate Challenge Fund, Community Growing Fund, Creative Scotland, Finnis Scott Foundation, Groundwork, and Grow Wild. Many thanks to the Aberdeenshire Environmental Fo-

rum for awarding the Green Butterfly Award to Huntly Town, partly in recognition of the work of the *Town is the Garden* project. The award gave the team great encouragement.

We would like to thank everyone who took part in the *Town is the Garden* project, for their generosity, patience and support. In particular those who contributed to the programme: Matt Aitkenhead, Andy Smith, Charlie Ashton, Grace Banks, Rosa Bevan and James Reid, John Bolland, Stephen Brandes, Alan Carter, Karen Collins, Doug Cookson, Uist Corrigan, Bob Donald, David Easton and Jane Lockyer, Petra/Patrick Geddes, Katrina Flad, Marguerite Fleming, Vicky Flood, David Foubister, Cristina Grasseni, Charlie Hanks, Margaret and Andrew Lear, Leslie Mabon, John Malster, Ann Miller, Miranda Montgomery, Bryan Morrison, Joshua Msika, Lorna Patterson, Chris Pepper, Annabel Pinker, Ian Scott, Pat Scott, Christine Steiner, Emma Stewart, Katie Stewart, Andrew Tassell, Leanne Townsend, Nikki and James Yoxall, David Watts, the Grow it, Cook it, Eat it team at BBC Radio Scotland, and everyone at the Scottish Sculpture Workshop.

And finally to Yvonne Billimore, Richard Muscat and Mariuccia Muscat, for all kinds of care, encouragement, sharp-eyes and support throughout.

Town is the Garden Chapbooks: Seeds
Published by Deveron Projects and Intellect in 2021

Edited by Joss Allen and Caroline Gatt
Layout by Joss Allen
Cover illustrations by Jamie Johnson
Printed and bound by Footprint Workers Cooperative, Leeds

Typeface: Adobe Casion Pro / Garamond Pro
Paper: Context Natural / Evercopy Plus

ISBN 978-1-907115-37-0

Deveron Projects is a company limited by guarantee, registered
in Scotland No. SC391020 and a registered Scottish Charity
No. SC024261

Town is the Garden Chapbooks
Deveron Projects and Intellect

Story II
/
Joss Allen and Elisabetta Rattalino

Story II

Art and agriculture: A tale in four seasons
Elisabetta Rattalino

Town is the Garden is down with the worms
Joss Allen

Art and agriculture: A tale in four seasons
Elisabetta Rattalino

AUTUMN
Ploughing: Turn up the earth (of an area of land) with a plough, especially before sowing.

Rome, 1973. Artist Gianfranco Baruchello (b.1924) lives with his family a few kilometres north of Rome, on the road to the town of Formello. He has just moved to evade the capital's turmoil—at the time, left-wing militants like him fear prosecution for recent terrorist attacks. He has no experience with farming but he decides to plough the abandoned fields that surround his property as a kind of performative action. This action inaugurates eight years of exceptional artistic experimentation that he will discuss in his book titled *How to Imagine. A Narrative on Art, Agriculture and Creativity* (1985), written with critic Henry Martin.

His point of reference is land art, the art practice of working directly in the landscape. Started in the USA in the mid-1960s, it soon became known in Italy thanks to art critics Germano Celant's and Tommaso Trini's reviews in architecture magazines. In September 1969, a documentary photograph of Dennis Oppenheim's *September Wheat* is in the pages of *Domus*. The image is an aerial view of a Dutch field being harvested in the form of an

X (Trini, 1969, 53). Oppenheim equates seeding and cultivating with making pigments for a painting.[1] For Oppenheim the land is a canvas.

Baruchello does not share Oppenheim's understanding of agricultural activities. On the contrary, he contests it and intervenes to react to it. He comments: "the disturbing thing about land art is that it is so completely aesthetic and all on a such a wrong scale. Anything that is enormous doesn't make any sense anymore if it's entirely without awareness of the social realities inside of which and all around which it operates […] I mean in Rome… at a time, when there wasn't enough money and determination to build new schools and housing" (Baruchello and Martin, 1983).

Bringing the fields of the Roman countryside back to their agricultural use has a political meaning to Baruchello. They have been abandoned due to inefficient land management regulations. A few years earlier, the municipality allowed urban dwellers to buy this agricultural land for building countryside villas. Soon after their acquisitions,

1. See the artist's statement in Tate acquisition file, https://www.tate.org.uk/art/artworks/oppenheim-directed-seeding-cancelled-crop-t12402.

the rules changed again: the new regulations returned the land to its agricultural purpose. At this point, in 1973, the plots are individually too small and collectively too expensive for farmers. Current landowners are unable to sell or profit. Denied their dreamed rural escapes, they forget these fields leaving them uncultivated. By occupying and putting the land to use again, Baruchello attempts to overcome this administrative impasse, to produce food and to prevent fires in the area during the hottest days of the year. Originally an urban dweller himself, he is now well-aware of farmers' ecological role as environmental stewards.

It is another young Italian artist, Giuseppe Penone, who finds associations between farming, land-management activities and (land) art. "My grandfather, for instance, used to make wonderful works of art. These are some: a road carved into rocks for 500 metres alongside the riverbed of the Rio Manico to connect the wood to the municipal road; removal and burial of boulders to use a piece of land as a meadow; grafting around 1500 trees; rerouting of the river Rio Manico to gain a cultivable area; annual harvesting of around 16000 square meters of land," he comments in an interview about Arte Povera with art critic Mirella Bandini in 1972 (Bandini, 1972, 66).

WINTER

Home-growing: The action or activity of growing something at home, on one's own land, or in one's own country.

Huston, March 1972. The highly-criticised exhibition 10 curated by Adler Sebastian inaugurates the new Contemporary Arts Museum in Huston (Adler, 1972). As part of the exhibition, movable containers occupy a hundred square metres of the main building. They host potatoes, peas, beans, carrots, lettuces, tomatoes, onions and few fruit trees. *Portable Farm*—the title of this installation—is Newton Harrison's *Survival Piece VI* (Ibid., 14–19).

The series started in 1971, when the artist positioned *Survival Piece II* in front of the entrance of LACMA, Los Angeles County Museum of Art (Ryan, 2015). Collaborating with scientists as part of the museum's Art and Technology programme, the artist reproduced the simplest of ecosystems in four water-filled tanks: Dunaliella Salina algae and Artemia brine shrimps. The ever-changing eco-systemic configuration was a spectacle for the viewers' aesthetic appreciation. After *Survival Piece II* and over the following two years, the growing awareness of the planet's deteriorating environmental conditions led Harrison to develop works around nutrition in times of limited resources—how will we feed the world's growing population? *Portable Farm* responds to and raises questions around this concern.

A few months after Harrison's work is installed in Huston, Argentinian artist Louis Fernando Benedit brings a hydroponic greenhouse, *Phitotron*, to MoMA, the Museum of Modern Art in New York (Ezcurra, 2019).[2] Started in the mid-1960s, the artist's research is not concerned with environmental questions. Instead, following critic Jorge Glusberg's idea of "arte de sistemas", it aims at dismantling the traditional notion of a finished art object in favour of designing *processes*. As part of his practice, the artist conceives complex, maze-like artificial environments for animals (for bees, ants, mice, for instance) to trigger new behaviours and relations among them. *Phitotron* does not include animals. It is a wide structure that hosts seventy tomato plants and fifty-six lettuces, bathed with artificial light and nurtured with a chemical compound. In the museum, the hydroponic garden

2. See *Projects: Luis Fernando Benedit*. November 14, 1972–January 2, 1973.

loses its productive purpose. It becomes a display device for organic processes and living artificial ecosystems.

Just a few months before Benedit's exhibition, the Museum awarded a prize to an Italian radical designers' collective, Gruppo 9999, for their proposal titled *Vegetable Garden House*. As part of Emilio Ambasz's *Italy: The New Domestic Landscape* (26 May – 11 September 1972), the award for emerging talents accompanies the exhibition of 120 signature design objects and nine environments (Ambasz, 1972). Presented as a series of collages, their domestic greenhouse brings organic life and its mystique in the modern home. Vegetables are food for the body. Attending to organic growth nurtures the soul.

13

SPRING

To Plant: Put (a seed, bulb, or plant) in the ground so that it can grow.

Chicago, May 1993. Walking on Greenleaf Street in the northern area of Chicago, a passer-by can glimpse into the window at No. 1769, and see a hydroponic garden. Leafy vegetables are growing beneath the cold glare of ultra-violet lights. Sprouts of Swiss chard, mustard, kale, and collard greens line up on plant stands made of screwed metal and wooden pipes, or hang in metal strap hangers. This indoor cultivation is an art intervention, one of the eight projects that are developed thanks to the ground-breaking public-art programme run by curator Mary Jane Jacob, *Culture in Action*. New Public Art in Chicago (Olson, Brenson and Jacob, 1995).

The event invites artists to intervene in neighbourhoods of the city, engaging with communities living locally to participate in their projects. Local artists' collective *Haha* (Richard House, Wendy Jacob, Laurie Palmer, John Ploof) initiate a group of over twenty people named Flood, with the idea to create a community garden.[3] This initial idea evolves into the hydroponic farm on Greenleaf Street.

Flood's garden means to respond to the contemporary AIDS crisis—a crisis that the artists have experienced first-hand. Gardening can be therapeutic in different ways: as a sort of nurturing therapy for people isolated because of their illness; providing an alternative source of nutrition for people HIV- and AIDS-positive. The vegetables selected for the garden are rich in beta-carotene, a pigment with antioxidant properties.

A caring community soon emerges from and gravitates around the intervention in the store. Once the hydroponic cultivation was up and running, networks for distributing the vegetables to local clinics were organised, along with regular discussions on safe sex, caring for people with AIDS, hydroponic gardening and how to get the word out. By the end of the summer, the group had also designed several in-home hydroponic gardening units that could be made from readily available hardware store materials.

3. See http://www.hahahaha.org/projFlood.html.

Prior to the publication of Bourriaud's *Relational Aesthetics* (1998), critics already recognised the aesthetic dimension of the project in the appearance of the garden and in its symbolic echoes. "The greens were at once vibrant and delicate, hearty and thread-like, patients themselves in a spic-and-span plant ward", Joseph Scanlan writes in *Frieze*; "The more one looked, the more the metaphor of the plants as patients on a nutrient-enriched, group IV became evident, and yet this metaphor of illness and maintenance was deferred by Flood's extroverted objective" (Scanlan, 1993). Yet, Jacob's initiative, and Flood's project specifically, can be framed within Susanne Lacy's idea of "New Genre Public Art" (1995), one that entails particular care to artists' relationships with "the audience" in every phase of a project (Lacy (ed.), 1995). Cultivating is caring.

SUMMER

Dogdays: The hottest period of the year (reckoned in antiquity from the heliacal rising of Sirius, the Dog Star).

Huntly, 2017. In the rural Scottish town of Huntly, an artist, Joss Allen, an architect, Camille Sineau, and a gardener, Lindy Young, initiate the *Town is the Garden*, a project that uses gardening to create a more sustainable local food economy for the town. This project is promoted by the socially-engaged arts organisation Deveron Projects and funded by the Climate Challenge Fund. The team starts to grow a vegetable garden and fruit trees for public use in the back garden of the Brander Building, where the organisation has its headquarter. But it also offers their labour, knowledges and resources to people living locally, helping, designing, sowing, planting, weeding and harvesting new vegetable and herbs gardens across the town.

Over the next twelve months, the community involved in the project expands. The project's team expands too: an anthropologist, Caroline Gatt, joins in; artists participate in the programme; new project interns support the activities.[4] Organising monthly-skills workshops, seed-exchange sessions, gatherings with local growers and initiating a resource library, the *Town is the Garden* nurtures and regenerate the food-growing culture in a rural town that seems, at times, to neglect the benefits of domestic and small-scale agriculture. It also fosters an alternative economy for food sharing by hosting a "barter shop" in the town centre.

The *Town is the Garden* is one of the initiatives that, in recent years, have been developed by/with artists or creative practitioners in rural areas. As Casa delle Agricolture Tullia e Gino, it is one of the few that engages with agriculture. Casa delle Agricolture Tullia e Gino is a grass-roots voluntary association officially started by a diverse group of practitioners that includes farmers, artists, activists, journalists, economists, in a village in southern Italy, Castiglione d'Otranto.[5] Named after the Italian pioneers of organic agriculture, the association aims to actively promote agrobiodiversity.

4. For an extended list of project contributors, see "Town is the Garden is down with the worms" in this chapbook.
5. See https://www.casadelleagricultureturulliaegino.com/.

Since 2012, the association has taken over fifteen hectares of abandoned land that is now redistributed free of charge to local growers; has initiated a biodiversity nursery to recover lost plant species; it runs a school for agriculture; it promotes campaigns against the use of pesticides. Every summer, they organise a convivial event titled *La Notte Verde (The Green Night)*, to raise awareness about environmental issues. Despite their differences, these two projects explore alternative economies and ecologies of co-existence around agriculture. As every other professional, artists contribute with their skills to the emergence of vibrant communities.

Political theorist Anthony Giddens writes about the paradox between the awareness of the dramatic future looming over humanity, and our human inability to do little or anything to change the course of the events that are rushing us towards an irreparable environmental crisis (Giddens, 2009). Of course, artist' work can bring climate change concerns to the public sphere and discourse. But they also get involved and contribute to action: small-scale, collaborative, organic growing is—possibly—a way to do so.

References

Adler, Sebastian (ed.). *10* (Huston: Contemporary Arts Museum, 1972).

Ambasz, Emilio (ed.), *Italy: the new domestic landscape achievements and problems of Italian design* (New York: The Museum of Modern Art, 1972).

Bandini, Mirella. *1972. Arte Povera a Torino* (Turin: Allemandi & C, 2002).

Baruchello, Gianfranco., and Martin, Henry. *How to Imagine: a narrative on art and agriculture* (New York: McPherson, 1983).

Casa delle Agriculture Tullia e Gino. https://www.casadelleagriculturetulliaegino.com/

Ezcurra, Mara Polgovsky. "The Future of Control: Luis Fernando Benedit's Labyrinths Series". *Post-Notes for an art in global context* (2019). https://post.at.mo-ma.org/profiles/995-mara-polgovsky-ezcurra

Giddens, Anthony. *The Politics of Climate Change*

(Cambridge: Polity, 2009).

Haha. http://www.hahahaha.org/projFlood.html

Lacy, Suzanne(ed.). *Mapping the Terrain: New Genre Public Art* (Seattle: Bay Press, 1995).

Oppenheim, Dennis. *Directed Seeding - Cancelled Crop (1969)* [Artist's statement]. Tate acquisition file. Accessed online. https://www.tate.org.uk/art/artworks/oppenheim-directed-seeding-can-celled-crop-t12402

Olson, Eva M., Brenson, Michael., and Jacob, Mary Jane. *Culture in Action* (Seattle: Bay Press, 1995).

Ryan, Leslie. "Performing agriculture: The 'Survival Pieces' of artists Helen and Newton Harrison" [conference paper]. Association for Environmental Studies and Sciences conference 2015. Accessed online. https://www.researchgate.net/publication/291559175_Performing_agriculture_The_Survival_Pieces_of_artists_Helen_and_Newton_Harrison

Scanlan, Joseph. "Culture in Action. Sculpture

Chicago" *Frieze* (5 November 1993). Accessed online. https://www.frieze.com/article/culture-action

Trini, Tommaso. "The Prodigal Maker's Trilogy", Domus 471 (Sept. 1969).

23

Town is the Garden is down with the worms
Joss Allen

After three years of thinking and making with the garden, we're returning to the compost heap. From this incredible heap we first emerged, and began with a party![1] In glasshouses, allotments, orchards and empty shops we planned gardens together, crafting *gardens of possibilities* and *possible gardens of kinship.*[2]

While our first seeds were germinating, we went foraging *food for free.*[3] We found rhubarb, planted along railway lines long ago, and elderflower every-where—intoxicated by their heady scent we began our dance with the seasons. Through the *seasons of weeds*, we learned stories from plants in all the wrong places and became collaborators in contam-inating diversity.[4] Weeds followed us wherever we

---

1. *Plant Party* #1 with Uist Corrigan, David Foubister, Miranda Montgomery, James Reid (Tap O' Noth Farm), David Ross (Glamourhaugh allotments) and Ian Scott (Strathbogie Horticultural Society) 17/06/17; The Incredible Heap 22/07/17.
2. *A Garden of Possibilities* 08/03/18; *Possible Gardens of Kinship* with Alexandra Falter and James Reid 16/06/18.
3. *Food fir Free,* 24/05/17; *Food fir Free,* 28/06/17; *Food fir Free* with Leanne Townsend (Wild Food Stories), 08/09/19.
4. *Seasons of Weeds: Spring* with Eleanor Brown, John

went and we followed them. *From little or nothing*, we found companionship with mushrooms and they showed us abundance from waste.[5] Again we partied.[6]

Mapping the soils of Huntly, we travelled through *communities from below*, composting as we went.[7] Singing "we are all compost, citizens of decay and lovers of worms!"[8] *From old ways with new hands* we wove stories and memory together into gathering baskets for harvests still to come.[9] We practiced *thinking like a forest*, performing possible paths towards more-than-human communicative habits.[10] In the *queer garden of abundant possibilities*, we considered what practices of tending towards or tending for plants can teach us about how we pay

Malster and Elisabetta Rattalino, 24/03/18; See Tsing (2012, 95–97).

5. *From Little or Nothing* with Ann Miller (Ann for Fungi), 14/04/18.

6. *Plant Party #2* with Katrina Flad (Frock n Wellies) 19/05/18

7. *Communities from Below* with Matt Aitkenhead (The James Hutton Institute), 21/07/18.

8. See Haraway, 2015, 161.

9. *From Old Ways with New Hands* with Karen Collins (Naturally Useful), 18/08/18.

10. *Thinking Like a Forest* with Alan Carter (Scottish Forest Garden) and Caroline Gatt, 23/02/19

attention to our surroundings and to one another.[11] In fallow months we were glad to have bread! We found companionship through kneading yeasty communities of saccharomyces cerevisiae with our own.[12] With humour and hopefulness, we cooked our way through a cataclysm.[13] Again we partied.[14]

We gathered round the *future hairst*, fomenting and fermenting with microbial cultures.[15] In the

11. *Queer Garden of Abundant Possibilities* with Eleanor Brown and Joe Crowdy 15/06/19.

12. *As long as there is bread* with Doug Cookson (Crannach Bakery), Charlie Hanks (Granton Community Bakery) and Katy Stewart ("The Macduff Loaf"), 16–17/03/19. Companion from "with (*cum*) bread (*pan*)".

13. *Cooking in a Cataclysm* with Stephen Brandes (Domestic Godless) 06/09/19. The menu included: "a post-industrial swathe of tidal estuary turned into a nutritious and moreish cup-a-soup, an agricultural pest selectively bread into a rare gastronomic delicacy (aquatic rabbit with foraged mushrooms), followed by 'one-hundred Gauloises' cigarette-ash ice-cream. Served alongside an alcopop designed to thwart an unwanted population boom and combat predatory sexual behaviour in men."

14. *Plant Party #3* with Christine Borland, Katrina Flad and Christine Steiner 18/05/19.

15. Hairst is doric (the dialect of northeast Scotland) for harvest. Huntly Hairst with Bob Donald (One Seed Forward), Lorna Patterson (NFU), James Reid

town square we assembled, plotted and dreamed, *beyond local* and global, of regenerative agriculture and diverse food economies.[16] We feasted on pit-fired vegetables cooked in the earth. We travelled round the table and round the world, sharing stories of and with food, from local to global and back again.[17] When the harvest was bountiful, whatever surplus we had, we gifted, swapped or shared.[18] An alternative economy in an empty shop; we bartered: one cabbage for five apples, half a dozen duck eggs for three lucky charms, the promise of a story for a beetroot or two. [19] Courgettes became chutney, blackcurrants sweetened to jam, fireweed tamed and dried into tea. Oh how life gave us apples! Many hands pressed them into juice, into cider, into vinegar, into a tradition.[20] Preserving the

and David Watts (Aberdeen University), 02/09/17; Huntly Hairst with Eleanor Brown 01/09/18.

16. *Beyond Local: Alternative Food Economies* with Cristina Grasseni (University of Leiden), Emma Stewart and David Foubister, 01/09/18; *People's Assembly* with John Bolland and Nikki Yoxall (Huntly Climate Action), 07/09/19.

17. *Global Potlatch Dinner,* 01/09/18.

18 *Gift/Swap/Share* (summer to autumn 2017) at 11 Gordon St.

19. The Barter Shop (2018–20) at 8 Castle St.

20. Yearly community apple pressing at the Huntly

bounty; but not the past.

After we had our fill of the harvest, we made plans for the next. Conspiring with seeds against those who would patent and privatise earthly knowledge.[21]

In the orchard, we became entangled with *future fruit*, reanimating and rethinking with Patrick Geddes towards a multispecies commons.[22] With Geddes we walked through deep time to the future now, from *aeons to apple trees*.[23] Oh how we got cosmic and biodiverse! Across generations we told stories in the orchard; ate, drank and celebrated what it, *they*, had given us.[24] With care we tended

farmers' market with the support of David Easton, Jane Lockyer and Bryan Morrison.

21. *Seed Savers Café* with Charlie Ashton and Joshua Msika (The James Hutton Institute), 30/09/17; *Seed Saving Walk* with John Malster. 02/09/18.

22. *Future Fruit* with Jonathan Baxter and Sarah Gittins 2019–20.

23. *Aeons and Apple Trees* with Petra/Patrick Geddes, John Malster, Helen Rowe (Aberdeenshire Council Ranger Service) and Fi Thomson, 17/08/19. Organised with Jonathan Baxter and Sarah Gittins.

24. *Apple day picnic* with Grace Banks and residents from the Meadows Carehome and staff, 21/08/18; *Graft* with Andrew Lear Andrew Lear, Annie Lord and Neep & Okra Kitchen, organised with Jonathan Baxter and Sarah Gittins, 08/02/20. On pronouns

to broken branches and rabbit-bitten boles, and coaxed the trees into another year of harvest.[25] Carrier bags full of apples, crap apples, greengages, plums, damsons, medlars, and a handful of hazel nuts. The orchard had it all ... but not quite. Something was missing. With commoners, sharp knives and gifted scions we grafted new trees for a hopeful future.[26]

In the morning over breakfast, with bleary eyes, we made *field notes for surviving the future*, on the entanglement of human and more-than-human worlds, matters of care, uncommoning nature, queer nature, lichens, learning to die in the Anthropocene, carrier bag theories, and world-wise otherwise stories.[27] We speculated an ecology, otherwise—we stepped towards other

for plants, see "Learning the Grammar of Animacy" in Kimmerer (2013, 48–59).

25. *Caring for Trees* with Vicky Flood and Chris Pepper, 24/08/18; Orchard maintenance with Johnny Barton and James Yoxall; Future Fruit Pruning workshop with Andrew Lear, 30/11/19.

26. See Bollier (2014) for "commoners"; *Graft*; and see Huntly Community Orchard, https://www.facebook.com/groups/2908085872645021/

27. *FN-SF: Fieldnotes on Surviving the Future* reading group (2018–20); the reading group was preceded by a series of talks in 2017 that included contributions from Leslie Mabon (University of the Highlands and Islands) and Annabel Pinker (The James Hutton Institute).

ecological ways of being. We learned the arts of living on a damaged planet.[28] Over lunch we honed our skills and practice as gardeners, eyes fixed on the ground.[29] In the evenings, with eyes open wide, we journeyed across worlds to other ecosystems and other ways of knowing.[30]

Whatever seeds we had saved, we gifted; whatever knowledge we had gathered, we shared.[31]

Now back to the heap, back to the earthworms and their multispecies wonderland.[32] Let's see what emerges from the humus. ...

28. Tsing et al (2017).
29. *Gardeners' Lunch* led by Lindy Young.
30. For the full film programme, see https://www.deveron-projects.com/town-garden/.
31. In a very literal sense some of the seeds we gathered are beginning to germinate: the Strathbogie Seed Collective is an emerging seed library which grew out of the *Town is the Garden* project. Organised by its curators, Katrina Flad and Dawn Finch, the collective distributes heirloom, open-sourced, local and organic seed to its members, encouraging them to save their own seed, and return some of it back to the library to replenish its stock. Some of the knowledge we gathered can be accessed through the *Town is the Garden* library, part of Deveron Projects archive and ever growing collection of books, available for anyone to browse.
32. See Hamilton and Neimanis, n.d.

References

Haraway, Donna. "Anthropocene, Capitalocene, Plantationocene, Chthluluocene: Making Kin". *Environmental Humanities* 6 (2015). 161.

Hamilton, Jennifer Mae., and Neimanis, Astrid. "Composting Feminisms". *Composting Feminisms* (n.d.). Accessed online. https://compostingfeminisms.wordpress.com/about/

Kimmerer, Robin Wall. *Braiding Sweetgrass: Indigenous Wisdom, Scientific Knowledge and the Teaching of Plants* (Canada : Milkweed Editions, 2013), 48–59.

Tsing, Anna., Swanson, Heather Anne., Gan, Elaine., and Bubandt, Nils (eds.). *Arts of Living on a Damaged Planet: Ghosts and Monsters of the Anthropocene* (USA: University of Minnesota Press, 2017).

Tsing, Anna. "Contaminated Diversity in 'Slow Disturbance': Potential Collaborators for a Liveable Earth". In Gary Martin, Diana Mincyte, and Ursula Münster (eds.). *Why Do We Value Diver-*

sity? Biocultural Diversity in a Global Context, RCC Perspectives 9 (2012). 95–97

Joss Allen can be found at the edges of the garden, amongst the weeds and compost heaps. He is an art-worker and gardener exploring how creative practices can shape earthy politics, community economies and ecological ways of being in playful, radical, responsive and meaningful ways. He is interested in collaborations across disciplines, peer education, storytelling and community building. His work has been influenced by his time as a support worker for adults with autism, a labourer on an organic farm and a refuse collector, among others. Joss currently lives in Helsinki, Finland where he is in the process of establishing a local seed library and pursuing a PhD research project on seed saving and story.

Elisabetta Rattalino is a Postdoctoral Research Fellow at the Faculty of Design and Art of the Free University of Bolzano. She holds a PhD in Art History from the School of Art History of the University of St Andrews ("The Seasons in the City. Artists and Rural Worlds in the Era of Calvino and Pasolini", 2018). Her research focuses on artistic practices from 1945 to present day, with a special interest in Italian postwar art and primarily on issues related to art, environment and vernacular rural cultures. Since 2010, Elisabetta has been collaborating with socially-engaged artists and arts organisations in both Italy (Cittadellarte - Fondazione Pistoletto, Biella; Kaninchenhaus, Turin; BAU, Bolzano) and Scotland (Deveron Projects).

38

Town is the Garden

A community food growing project, *of sorts*.

For three years the Town is the Garden team could be found at the margins of the garden. Amongst the weeds and compost heaps, they explored what it might mean to *think with* the garden. Through crafting gardens, vegetable plots and orchards they attempted to rethink how a community might feed itself as it faces up to the global climate and ecological emergency. Through the processes of learning and sharing skills in relation to growing food, from planting seeds to preserving the harvest, they asked how we might also begin to pay better attention to the entanglement of human and more-than-human worlds. They asked how might the garden be a site of both resistance and resilience? A place for *thinking* and *doing* ecology, otherwise.

This is *Story II* in a collection of seven chapbooks by the *Town is the Garden* that attempt to capture some of the diverse ways of thinking, doing and knowing the project explored with some of the people they explored them with. It includes contributions from Eleanor Brown and Alexandra Falter (*Plants*), Jonathan Baxter & Sarah Gittins (*Orchard*), Joe Crowdy (*Garden*), Dawn Finch

(*Seeds*), Maria Puig de la Bellacasa (*Compost*), and Joss Allen, Caroline Gatt and Elisabetta Rattalino (*Story*). With cover illustrations by Jamie Johnson.

The Town is the Garden team included: Joss Allen (2017–20), Rhian Davies (2019–20), Caroline Gatt (2018–20), Camille Sineau (2017–18), and Lindy Young (2017–19).

https://www.deveron-projects.com/town-garden

The *Town is the Garden* team would like to thank everyone who contributed to these chapbooks and Footprint Workers Cooperative for their exceptional printing skills.

A massive thank you to everyone at Deveron Projects, staff, board and interns (too many to name), especially Petra Pennington, Robyn Wolsey and Claudia Zeiske—for their support and guidance—and the *Neep & Okra Kitchen* team—with whom we latterly shared space and ideas with. To Alex Severn, our wonderful intern, on a student placement from the University of Aberdeen. To our generous funders Aberdeenshire Council, Action Earth, Climate Challenge Fund, Community Growing Fund, Creative Scotland, Finnis Scott Foundation, Groundwork, and Grow Wild. Many thanks to the Aberdeenshire Environmental

Forum for awarding the Green Butterfly Award to Huntly Town, partly in recognition of the work of the *Town is the Garden* project. The award gave the team great encouragement.

We would like to thank everyone who took part in the *Town is the Garden* project, for their generosity, patience and support. In particular those who contributed to the programme: Matt Aitkenhead, Andy Smith, Charlie Ashton, Grace Banks, Rosa Bevan and James Reid, John Bolland, Stephen Brandes, Alan Carter, Karen Collins, Doug Cookson, Uist Corrigan, Bob Donald, David Easton and Jane Lockyer, Petra/Patrick Geddes, Katrina Flad, Marguerite Fleming, Vicky Flood, David Foubister, Cristina Grasseni, Charlie Hanks, Margaret and Andrew Lear, Leslie Mabon, John Malster, Ann Miller, Miranda Montgomery, Bryan Morrison, Joshua Msika, Lorna Patterson, Chris Pepper, Annabel Pinker, Ian Scott, Pat Scott, Christine Steiner, Emma Stewart, Katie Stewart, Andrew Tassell, Leanne Townsend, Nikki and James Yoxall, David Watts, the Grow it, Cook it, Eat it team at BBC Radio Scotland, and everyone at the Scottish Sculpture Workshop.

And finally to Yvonne Billimore, Richard Muscat and Mariuccia Muscat, for all kinds of care, encouragement, sharp-eyes and support throughout.

Town is the Garden: Story II
Published by Deveron Projects and Intellect in 2021

Edited by Joss Allen and Caroline Gatt
Layout by Joss Allen
Cover illustrations by Jamie Johnson
Printed and bound by Footprint Workers Cooperative, Leeds

Typeface: Adobe Casion Pro / Garamond Pro
Paper: Context Natural / Evercopy Plus

ISBN 978-1-907115-37-0

Deveron Projects is a company limited by guarantee, registered in Scotland No. SC391020 and a registered Scottish Charity No. SC024261

Garden

/

Joe Crowdy

Garden

Cultivating queer friendship
&
Rosy pink walls of trees and
bushes of the garden

Joe Crowdy

Cultivating queer friendship

[A] historiography powered by the connecting forces of desire, friendship and vegetal life; a way of living with others differently, powered by history and plants.

~ Joe Crowdy, this volume

In June 2019, I travelled to Aberdeenshire to deliver two workshops for Deveron Projects' *Town is the Garden* project.[1] These workshops offered the opportunity to share and develop ideas from my 2017 article, "Queer Undergrowth", which proposed a history of weeds as queer agents in the horticultural logic and social space of the garden.[2] In Huntly, I focused on three historical examples of gardens that cultivated queer intimacy, providing fertile ground for discussing our own relationships with, and amongst, plants. One workshop was open to the public, whilst the other was conducted with the local school's LGBTQ+ group, who were planning a new garden within the school grounds. These teenagers were an established gang: bonded through weekly meetings and shared experiences, they had created their own private space within the walls and routine of the school. Looking back on this welcoming atmosphere of good humour and

1. See https://www.deveron-projects.com/events/workshop-queer-ecologies/.
2. See Crowdy (2017), https://joecrowdy.com/Queer-Undergrowth.

camaraderie, I realise how reminiscent it was of the intimate spaces of queer friendship I went on to describe.

Whilst gardens are rife with sex between plants, and overgrown spaces have long been used for queer sexual encounters—think how cruisers use shaded shrubberies—I was interested in exploring a broader concept of intimacy. Rather than an identity label, sexuality here is a catch-all term for the tangled performance of desire, affection and attachment between friends, lovers, and strangers, which may lead to flirtation, pleasure, or, sometimes, nothing. As Elizabeth Grosz asserts, "our sexualities… are not one thing, but… mosaic like fields composed of aligned but disparate elements, energies, goals, wills…" (Grosz, 2005, 195). Sexual orientation is, in Sara Ahmed's words, "a matter of residence" (Ahmed, 2006, 1)—a question of how we inhabit space, and how space informs interaction. Flirtation is not only a prelude to sex, but also a form of platonic or intellectual intimacy. The classical Greek model of male friendship, as George Haggerty notes, was based on sensual appreciation of beauty and "intense personal affection" (Haggerty, 2019, 7), but also on dialogue and shared enjoyment of nature. Friendship—*philia*—

as a verb—*philein*—means both "to love" and "to make love". "Making love" does not have to mean sex, but rather the active making of something new through intimacy. At the turn of the twentieth century, this "concept of friendship offered a means whereby same-sex intimacy could be explored" (Ibid.,1), where love between friends could equal that of publicly identified couples.

I began each workshop by asking participants to describe their own emotional attachments to plants. I told them of Luce Irigaray's account of returning to the world of plants in times of emotional, social, and intellectual stress, gaining nourishment through "intimacy with the vegetal world" (Irigaray and Marder, 2016, 7). And I told them of my own attachment to stinging nettles—omnipresent plant of my childhood, raucous resident of every wasteland and riverbank, whose virile growth and astringent scent triggers memories of secret dens, games in the undergrowth, hot white bumps on red skin. By filling the room with their own memories, before I evoked more distant histories, I hoped participants would make connections between the two. The gardens I went on to describe epitomise a flirtatious mode of living with the past: a historiography powered by the connecting forces of de-

3

sire, friendship and vegetal life; a way of living with others differently, powered by history and plants.

Natalie Barney's queer garden salon at 20 Rue Jacob

My story began in author and salonnière Natalie Barney's secluded garden in Paris: an early twentieth-century hub for lesbian intimacy and literary debate. Barney's salon, according to Katarina Bonnevier, "operated through bodies and walls, conversations and costumes, furniture and intrigues" (Bonnevier, 2007, 374)—but also, we might add, through the limbs and lives of plants. Informed by Gottfried Semper's theory of textiles as the source of architectural enclosure, Bonnevier describes the salon's layering of screens and surfaces, which aimed not for modernist truth and purity, but enigma, romance. Architectural binaries, Bonnevier argues, were queered through the porous relationship between the salon's interior and the surrounding garden. Openings looked out onto dark tapestries of verdure, and foliage-filtered light slipped across rugs, upholstery and the limbs of lounging guests. In Barney's boudoir, walls covered in "pink damask, the color of flesh", enclosed visitors "on three sides;

[whilst]... on the fourth side… [were] the trees and bushes of the garden" (Ibid.,156). In a 1966 BBC interview, an elderly Barney stoops beneath these branches, running their leaves tenderly through her hand. Behind her, the salon—an expanse of trellis, mirror, and glass—reflects back the foliage of sycamores, false acacias, rhododendrons and ferns.

This space was one parcel of a tiny woodland spreading across several private gardens. Impossible to visit as a whole, "Le Bois Visconti" can only be seen in fragments—snatched glimpses from neighbouring apartments.[3] This enclosed copse is the last remaining never-built-upon fragment of once-rural land: a medieval water-meadow turned rubbish dump. A recent survey of trees lists various cultivated specimens—walnut, loquat and fig—but mainly self-colonising species, "essence de friche": ruderal, or wasteland plants.[4] In both its historical origins and its living flora, then, Barney's garden, whilst a locus for cosmopolitan life, retained an-

3. See Essevaz-Roulet (n.d.), https://www. ruevisconti.com/FauneEtFlore/LeBoisVisconti/ BoisVisconti.html.
4. Ibid. List of trees composed by "Phillipe Glwx., notre consultant en botanique des Jardins du Luxembourg", with supplementary info from Christian Chevalier.

ti-urban roots.

Hidden at the heart of a succession of built and growing veils, a Grecian temple dedicated to friendship formed a stage for "poetry readings, tableaux vivants, and political protests" (Bonnevier, 132). Barney spearheaded the transformation of ancient poet Sappho into an emblem of homoerotic friendship—"the most lasting virtue", in Barney's words, based on "a sense of loyalty, and of choice" .[5] The fragmentary nature of Sappho's extant work, Samuel Dorf argues, was central to its creative appropriation by Barney (Dorf, 2009, 304). Recitals of these fragments, performed by friends and lovers around smoking brasiers and broken columns, began in her previous—remarkably similar—garden in Neuilly. Sycamores provided a dense canopy over the lawn, and ivy shrouded the perimeter wall. This shadowy vegetation of a self-sown grove, it appears, was precisely what Barney needed to stimulate her Sapphic incantations, her nostalgic productions of queer intimacy.

5. See Natalie Barney interview with Miron Grindea (1996).

Growing queer heaven: Edward Carpenter at Millthorpe

I turned next to the home of gay rights activist Edward Carpenter and his partner George Merrill, built in the rolling countryside of Derbyshire in 1883 as a refuge from industrial life and Victorian morality. As he wrote in 1916, Carpenter—like Irigaray—had long found "consolation and an escape from the wounds of daily life in intercourse with Nature" (Carpenter, 1916, 26). His early sexuality was formed over privileged summer afternoons at Cambridge, "canoeing... [beneath] overhanging willows, or through beds of iris... or sitting long on some turfy bank with a friend" (Ibid., 76, 4). Haunted by an obscure, "partly sexual, partly religious" longing, hours spent in moonlit College gardens, Carpenter writes, were "the most pregnant of my then existence" (Ibid., 4). Encounters with radical ideas of friendship in art—Walt Whitman's poetry particularly—helped elucidate the repressed allure of male intimacy. On a visit to Rome, the ideals of masculine beauty and companionship encapsulated in Greek sculpture— "so remote from... commercialism and Christianity"—left with him "the seed of new conceptions of life" (Ibid., 67, 68). Later, he would set his notion of "homogenic love", of a specifically queer—or "Uranian"—temperament within a history of "thousands and thousands" of queer lives (Ibid., 96).

This seed only flourished after Carpenter became involved in politics and moved north to Sheffield, finally finding his *"natural habitat"* at Millthorpe (Ibid., 101–2). Like fellow romantic socialist, William Morris, Carpenter saw manual work—once removed from the alienating logic of waged labour—as a source of emancipatory power. His infatuation with rural working life ultimately settled on the figure of Merrill, whose nature "had grown... entirely out of his own roots", and in whom he recognised "a peculiar intimacy and mutual understanding" (Ibid., 104, 159). He was struck by a vision "...within me, of something like the bulb and bud, with short green blades, of a huge hyacinth just appearing above the ground... a sign... that my life had... at last taken root, and was beginning rapidly to grow" (Ibid., 105). Millthorpe was at once a haven from society and a welcoming home for a new society —"a *rendezvous* for all classes and conditions of society..." (Ibid., 163–4). It became a meeting place for "parsons and positivists... scythesmiths and surgeons..." (Ibid., 164), a salon for the discussion of Marx, women's rights, and eastern mysticism. Influencing both the work of notable figures, such as architect of Letchworth Garden City, Raymond Unwin, and the everyday relationships of visiting couples (straight and gay), Millthorpe demonstrated a new way of living with nature and one another (Ibid., 165). In one visit, Morris sat by the fire, gleefully reading aloud Richard Jefferies' depiction "of an utterly ruined and deserted London, gone down in swamps and malaria, with brambles and weeds spreading through slum streets and fashionable squares" (Ibid., 217).

Photographs show the stone façade of the house engulfed by climbers—ivy reaching towards windows, a drift of jasmine above the door. Parallel with the façade runs an unruly hedge, seemingly a series of shrubs merged into one composite, billowing lump. Tendrils and errant saplings reach up out of it, and its base softly melts into grass and weeds. A protective cage for fruit bushes or brassicas sits amongst lupins, red hot pokers and poppies. We see Merrill feeding a flock of hens, a riot of tall mulleins sprouting from the pecked dirt. This is not a garden snipped and strained into regimented order! In several images, figures inhabit the different rooms of the garden, lounging

9

amongst its foliage. In two photographs of an iron bench, partially swallowed by the hedge, gestures of affection are repeated but their authors switch places. Carpenter sits in the centre in both, first with his right hand on the thigh of close friend George Hukin, whilst Merrill drapes a hand on his opposite shoulder; and second with his left hand on the thigh of a third, unknown friend, his calf pressed against Merrill's shoulder, who now sits cross-legged on the grass. Here is a garden populated by the intimacy of friends and lovers; a place where plants and people are left to spread and lean against, and towards, one another.

At the root of platonic love, Haggerty notes, is Diotima's assertion that when a man meets a beautiful friend "he conceives and gives birth to what he has been carrying inside him for ages" (Diotima in Plato in Haggerty, 150). Carpenter, we can see, clearly understood his life and relationships in similar terms. Dianne Chisholm describes precisely such a "nonprocreative" creativity, through Deleuze and Guattari's concept of "involution" (Chisholm in Sandilands and Erickson, 2000, 219). Unlike evolution, enacted through sexual reproduction, involution is the creative force of the rhizome. We find just such a notion of non-reproductive conception in E.M. Forster's account of how he gained inspiration for his novel *Maurice* (1913-14). On a visit to Millthorpe, Merrill "touched my backside – gently and just above the buttocks… It seemed to go straight through the small of my back into my ideas… at that precise moment I had conceived" (Forster in Furbank, 2000, 219). The creative power of Carpenter and Merrill's relationship is perhaps best illustrated in Carpenter's description of Merrill's own words:

> On one occasion he was standing at the door of our cottage, looking down the garden brilliant in the sun, when a missionary sort of man arrived with a tract and wanted to put it in his hand. 'Keep your tract,' said George. 'I don't want it.' 'But don't you wish to know the way to heaven?' said the man. 'No, I don't,' was the reply, 'can't you see that *we're in heaven here* – we don't *want* any better than this, so go away! (Carpenter, 163)

11

Gardening loss and desire: Derek Jarman on Dungeness

Finally, I described the exposed shingle garden of artist and filmmaker Derek Jarman at Dungness: a place comparable to these older gardens in its relation to queer desire, nature, and history, but with an entirely different visual and vegetal character. I showed two sequences from Jarman's 1990 missive on loss and desire, *The Garden*, where stony flowerbeds act as a backdrop for queer activism, a stage for a theatrical bricolage of historical references performed by Jarman's friends, and an intimate realm of reciprocal tender care between humans and plants. I wanted to show the students that gardening could build both a political platform and a private paradise, that might look unlike any other garden they knew. Jarman's garden represents a creative relationship with memory and history: a place to indulge in nostalgia or critique, to bring fragments of the past back to the present—driftwood, industrial waste, lines of poetry or popular song. But it also represents a relationship with a physical site and ecological neighbourhood open to chance and collaboration, where Jarman both plays mother nature, and submits to the wild power of wind and salt and spray: where a fragile, fleeting authorship is shared between artist, weather, and vegetation.

Touching other worlds

After studying the gardens of Barney, Carpenter and Jarman, we went outside to explore these ideas in nearby green spaces. The content of each workshop from this point diverged, but they shared a common material frame: two billowing sheets of dyed fabric, made in an effort to conjure a tangible link to these histories. Like props or fake relics, these pink sheets emulated the rosy damask walls of Barney's boudoir. But they were also a personal, private citation. In the autumn of 2015, on a site visit to a Sussex farm where we were soon to exhibit together, a close friend and I spent an exasperating, relationship-testing night, with a third, older friend, struggling to keep torrential rain out of a makeshift tent. In the morning, whilst our clothes dried at the farmhouse, we silently collected tub-fulls of blackberries from the hedgerows, took turns mashing them with our feet, then boiled them over a camping gaz in the fixing liquor of our urine. Huddled in the caustic stench, we dyed a five-metre length of linen and hung it to dry from a nearby oak. Later, we filmed ourselves carrying this rosy sail up the steep blue grass slope of a meadow, jumping and dancing to avoid patches of wet nettles. This was an intensely intimate moment of friendship: sharing the same discomfort, exhaustion and excitement, we had literally stirred ourselves together, fixed our relationship into a physical material. Four years later, I remembered this as I re-performed the dying process alone, combining my urine with the oxalic acid of rhubarb leaves. Too early for blackberries, I collected rose petals, bay leaves, and the burgundy foliage of copper beeches—tall trees which paid me back for stealing their leaves with a deep graze on my thumb, which later leaked puss every time I plunged my hands into the dye. I brought the new panels of fabric to Huntly, and in each workshop, we hung them from branches to enclose temporary places to talk: a fleeting architecture of foliage, flesh and memory.[6]

With the student group, this became a space to

6. See "Rosy pink walls of trees and bushes of the garden" in this chapbook for a recipe on plant dyeing.

explore design ideas for their own garden. I asked them to discuss the activities it might host, the references it might express, how it might reflect their collective interests. I wanted them to consider the essential steps in planning any garden—understanding the material, environmental, and historical conditions of a site, choosing plants according to how their habits might match those of the garden's users, and deciding how much control and care the garden will require—but also how such steps could be approached from a specifically queer perspective. Could the garden be a way of cultivating queer friendships, challenging standards of good taste, or performing connections with queer histories: the garden as a mnemonic device?

With the second group, I tried a more speculative activity, exploring the intimate, reciprocal relationships between plant and human bodies. Gardens, I argue, are both records of accumulated attention, and places with the potential to shift our thinking about desire and care, lust and labour. After we had trodden a circle in a lush crop of ground elder beneath a beech at the boundary of town and woodland, and gathered inside our pink and green walls, I recited an account of my attempt, working as a gardener, to disentangle an old rambling

15

rose from a musty mass of ivy. In order to prune this ball of ivy, I had to climb right inside it, grope blindly along its hairy branches, half searching for joints where I could cut, half locking our embrace to stop myself from falling. I began to understand its internal structural logic and history of growth, from young exploratory vine to heaving morass, writ in aged wooden elbows. For a moment, the plant which I was destroying held my weight. My body and attention were entirely consumed within it, dependent on it. That evening, lying in bed, the outlines of my limbs were distorted by undulating new forms of bites and stings from the ivy's invertebrate inhabitants, strangely firm and tight to touch, as if not entirely my own.

I hoped, with the group, to reflect on Catriona Sandilands' speculation whether there are "ways in which some material relationships to plants… enact forms of living and relating that resist, interrupt, or at least cause friction within… heteropatriarchy" (Sandilands, 2017, 428). Chisholm suggests that nature writer Ellen Meloy's imagined sexual encounter with the flower of a prickly pear cactus achieves something akin to this—"an erotic-ethical affiliation between human and nonhuman life" (Chisholm, 360). Meloy asks what it is that the prickly pear desires, how it loves the basalt rock on which it grows. If I desire to be devoured by a ball of ivy, what does the ivy desire of me? To leave it alone? Or to become a support on which it can finally obtain its ultimate desire, to metamorphose from climber to shrub?

I asked the participants to take turns guiding a partner, eyes closed, towards an individual plant, and to introduce their partner's hand to that plant—taking care that they didn't damage it, or themselves. I asked those with their eyes closed to think of the plant as a body, and to describe to their partner the textures and shapes of its limbs and skin. Next, I asked them to analyse the plant visually: what was missed in the first encounter, what was now invisible? Finally, I asked the pairs to speculate on the place of their plant within a local economy of desire and attention. To what environmental qualities did it attend? How could they read this in the plant's habit, how it occupied the ground? How did it provide an inhabitable ground for other organisms? How had humans paid attention to it—was it planted or self-sown, pruned, fertilised, or bred in a certain way?

Back in our beech salon, one participant commented how few of these questions she could answer. Rather than suggesting a sensual assessment alone could satisfy such questions, my intention was to get the participants thinking differently about how they know plants. Michael Marder laments how, in European history, post-Linnaean "nominalism has been the prevalent method of thinking about plants" (Marder, 2013, 4). To know a plant often means to name it, to assign "it an exact place in a dead, albeit highly differentiated, system", transforming a unique individual organism into a mere example of its species. An encounter with a plant must not simply be an attempt to fit it into a human world, but rather an acknowledgement of *another* world. Whilst fundamentally inaccessible, we can try to bring this world closer through recognising, like Carpenter, its commonalities with our own—such as the shared plant and human capacity for growth, change, and decay (Ibid., 9). We can also recognise where plants surpass human capacities, admiring their "rootedness in a place", their incredible "attentiveness to what is going on around them... light, heat, moisture, movement, vibration…" (Marder in Irigaray and Marder, 117, 154). By engaging with plants as "participants in the ensemble of life, rather than a mesh of quantifiable objects of productive potentialities" we can gain "a richer sense of... [our] own bod[ies]... [and our own] thinking" (Ibid., 133, 152).

I was also interested in how these encounters with plants were mediated by a third, human, party; or, conversely, how the intimate experience of being guided by a human partner was mediated by a plant. I had first performed this exercise as a spontaneous gesture on a marshland boardwalk with my own partner. With absolute trust in each other's guidance, we took turns walking long stretches with our eyes closed. When the long-anticipated moment of contact finally came with the body of a plant, it almost felt like the glossy, rough, or downy surfaces I was touching were part of my partner's own body, or that the supple or stiff limbs were somehow of his world, not mine. In the woods of Huntly, I hoped that the mutual experience of this tactile activity would create some impression of the plant-mediated intimacy between friends I had described in the gardens of Carpenter, Barney, and Jarman.

References

Ahmed, Sara. *Queer Phenomenology: Orientations, Objects, Others* (Durham: Duke University Press, 2006).

Barney, Natalie. "Interview with Miron Grindea". *New Release*. BBC2 (26 May 1966).

Bonnevier, Katarina. *Behind Straight Curtains: Towards a Queer Feminist Theory of Architecture* (Stockholm: Axl Books, 2007).

Carpenter, Edward. *My Days and Dreams: Being Autobiographical Notes* (London: George Allen & Unwin Ltd., 1916).

Dorf, Samuel. "Seeing Sappho in Paris: Operatic and Choreographic Adaptations of Sapphic Lives and Myths". *Music in Art* 34:1/2 (2009).

Essevaz-Roulet, Baptiste. "Rubrique Vététal". *Rue Visconti* (n.d.). Accessed online. https://www.ruevisconti.com/FauneEtFlore/LeBoisVisconti/BoisVisconti.html

Forster, E.M. "Terminal Note". In P. N. Furbank (ed.). *Maurice* (Harmondsworth: Penguin, 2000).

Grosz, Elizabeth. *Time Travels: Feminism, Nature, Power* (Durham: Duke University Press, 2005).

Haggerty, George E. *Queer Friendship: Male Intimacy in the English Literary Tradition* (Cambridge: Cambridge University Press, 2019).

Irigaray, Luce., and Marder, Michael. *Through Vegetal Being: Two Philosophical Perspectives* (New York: Columbia University Press, 2016).

Marder, Michael. *Plant-Thinking: A Philosophy of Vegetal Life* (New York: Columbia University Press, 2013).

Mortimer Sandilands, Catriona., and Erickson, Bruce (eds.). *Queer Ecologies: Sex, Nature, Politics, Desire* (Bloomington: Indiana University Press, 2010).

Sandilands, Catriona. "Fear of a Queer Plant?". *GLQ: A Journal of Lesbian and Gay Studies* 23:3 (2017).

*Rosy pink walls of trees and
bushes of the garden*

The walls are covered in pink damask, the color of flesh, the silk is fastened to the walls with panels and frames... the rosy pink walls enclose them on three sides; to their right, on the fourth side, are the trees and bushes of the garden.

~Katarina Bonnevier, *Behind Straight Curtains*, 2007

In love, 'tis equal measure. The Victor lives with empty pride, The Vanquisht dye with pleasure.

~Earl of Rochester, *Poems on Several Occasions*, 1701

Step 1: Make yourself (into) a mordant

Collect your urine (or the urine of a loved one) for a few days, until you have enough to fully submerge your fabric. Leave until stale and pungent.

Alternatively, gather enough rhubarb leaves to fill a large saucepan (not one you use for food!), chop into small pieces, cover with water, and boil for one hour.[7] Be careful not to breathe in the oxalic acid fumes. Cool, strain, discard the leaves, and reserve the liquor.

Step 2: Prepare your dye

Collect your pigment. The leaves of copper beech trees (Fagus sylvatica f. purpurea) and the petals of magenta roses (e.g. Rosa rugosa 'Roseraie de l'Hay') both contain the same pink pigment. Obtain the darkest, most richly coloured material possible – in the case of the copper beech, this

7. You could use the stems for a crumble to eat within your pink walls—mix with a bramley apple and raspberries, then cover with a crumble mix of 3 parts flour, 3 parts ground almonds, 4 parts butter, 2 parts sugar.

often means the leaves at the crown of the tree, so be prepared to climb. If you'd like a peachier tone, yellow pigment can be obtained from the leaves of bay trees (Lauris nobilis), or the inner bark of birch trees (Betula pendula); mix with your pink dye as desired. The higher the ratio of plant material to the weight of fabric, the richer the colour.

Chop your plant material into small pieces, cover with water, and leave overnight.

Heat your plant matter broth to a low boil, and leave to simmer for around an hour. Beech leaves will produce a surprisingly fruity aroma; rose petals will quickly lose their musky scent; bay leaves will smell like Christmas. Leave to cool. Strain, and discard the leaves, petals, or bark. The dye can be brightened a little by adding lemon juice.

Step 3: Prepare your fabric

If your budget allows, silk damask, as a natural protein-based fibre, would dye nicely. Alternatively, use any other white, natural fibre fabric (cotton, linen, wool). Wash your fabric after purchase to remove any factory treatment.

Submerge your fabric in your chosen mordant (or combination thereof), bring to the boil, and simmer for one hour. Leave to cool, strain, and rinse thoroughly in fresh water. The mordant coaxes the fabric into a more receptive mood for dyeing.

Step 4: Dye

Submerge your mordanted fabric into your dye in a large saucepan (the greater the quantity of fabric, the larger the pan will need to be, unless you are happy with patchy results). Add a generous cup of salt. Bring to a low boil, and simmer for around one hour. Leave to cool, drain, and hang your fabric to dry.

Once dry, iron your rosy pink walls of trees and bushes to help set the dye.

Joe Crowdy is a PhD fellow at the Oslo School of Architecture and Design, where he studies the architecture of the Cambridgeshire Fens at the cusp of seventeenth century drainage and enclosure, through the voices of those who inhabited and built this soon-to-be-devastated environment. He previously worked as an artist and gardener in the UK, and these practices continue to inform his research, both within and beyond his academic work.

Town is the Garden

A community food growing project, *of sorts*.

For three years the Town is the Garden team could be found at the margins of the garden. Amongst the weeds and compost heaps, they explored what it might mean to *think with* the garden. Through crafting gardens, vegetable plots and orchards they attempted to rethink how a community might feed itself as it faces up to the global climate and ecological emergency. Through the processes of learning and sharing skills in relation to growing food, from planting seeds to preserving the harvest, they asked how we might also begin to pay better attention to the entanglement of human and more-than-human worlds. They asked how might the garden be a site of both resistance and resilience? A place for *thinking* and *doing* ecology, otherwise.

This is *Garden* in a series of seven chapbooks by the *Town is the Garden* that attempt to capture some of the diverse ways of thinking, doing and knowing the project explored with some of the people they explored them with. It includes contributions from Eleanor Brown and Alexandra Falter (*Plants*), Jonathan Baxter & Sarah Gittins (*Orchard*), Joe Crowdy (*Garden*), Dawn Finch (*Seeds*), Maria Puig de la

Bellacasa (*Compost*), and Joss Allen, Caroline Gatt and Elisabetta Rattalino (*Story*). With cover illustrations by Jamie Johnson.

The Town is the Garden team included: Joss Allen (2017–20), Rhian Davies (2019–20), Caroline Gatt (2018–20), Camille Sineau (2017–18), and Lindy Young (2017–19).

https://www.deveron-projects.com/town-garden

The *Town is the Garden* team would like to thank everyone who contributed to these chapbooks and Footprint Workers Cooperative for their exceptional printing skills.

A massive thank you to everyone at Deveron Projects, staff, board and interns (too many to name), especially Petra Pennington, Robyn Wolsey and Claudia Zeiske—for their support and guidance—and the Neep & Okra Kitchen team—with whom we latterly shared space and ideas with. To Alex Severn, our wonderful intern, on a student placement from the University of Aberdeen. To our generous funders Aberdeenshire Council, Action Earth, Climate Challenge Fund, Community Growing Fund, Creative Scotland, Finnis Scott Foundation, Groundwork, and Grow Wild. Many thanks to the Aberdeenshire Environmental Fo-

32

rum for awarding the Green Butterfly Award to Huntly Town, partly in recognition of the work of the *Town is the Garden* project. The award gave the team great encouragement.

We would like to thank everyone who took part in the *Town is the Garden* project, for their generosity, patience and support. In particular those who contributed to the programme: Matt Aitkenhead, Andy Smith, Charlie Ashton, Grace Banks, Rosa Bevan and James Reid, John Bolland, Stephen Brandes, Alan Carter, Karen Collins, Doug Cookson, Uist Corrigan, Bob Donald, David Easton and Jane Lockyer, Petra/Patrick Geddes, Katrina Flad, Marguerite Fleming, Vicky Flood, David Foubister, Cristina Grasseni, Charlie Hanks, Margaret and Andrew Lear, Leslie Mabon, John Malster, Ann Miller, Miranda Montgomery, Bryan Morrison, Joshua Msika, Lorna Patterson, Chris Pepper, Annabel Pinker, Ian Scott, Pat Scott, Christine Steiner, Emma Stewart, Katie Stewart, Andrew Tassell, Leanne Townsend, Nikki and James Yoxall, David Watts, the Grow it, Cook it, Eat it team at BBC Radio Scotland, and everyone at the Scottish Sculpture Workshop.

And finally to Yvonne Billimore, Richard Muscat and Mariuccia Muscat, for all kinds of care, encouragement, sharp-eyes and support throughout.

Town is the Garden Chapbooks: Garden
Published by Deveron Projects and Intellect in 2021

Edited by Joss Allen and Caroline Gatt
Layout by Joss Allen
Cover illustrations by Jamie Johnson
Proofreading by Yvonne Billimore and Claudia Zeiske
Printed and bound by Footprint Workers Cooperative, Leeds

Typeface: Adobe Casion Pro / Garamond Pro
Paper: Context Natural / Evercopy Plus

ISBN 978-1-907115-37-0

Deveron Projects is a company limited by guarantee, registered
in Scotland No. SC391020 and a registered Scottish Charity
No. SC024261

Town is the Garden Chapbooks
Deveron Projects and Intellect

Story I
/
Joss Allen and Caroline Gatt

Story I

Prologue: Story seeds the garden
Joss Allen and Caroline Gatt

Introduction / Storying the development of the Town is the Garden
Joss Allen and Caroline Gatt

Prologue: Story seeds the garden
Joss Allen and Caroline Gatt

If gardens are also worlding projects, we can ask, not only what worlds are we cultivating in our gardens, but also, what worlds are our gardens designed to reproduce? Into which futures are we taking root?

~Natasha Myers, 2007

How might we cultivate in our gardens the kinds of stories necessary to flourish in these times?

In one of our monthly reading groups (*Field Notes on Surviving the Future*, "Speculative Fictions", 13/03/19) we encountered Ursula K Le Guin's essay, *The Carrier Bag Theory of Fiction*, in which she draws our attention, via Elisabeth Fisher's *Woman Creations*, towards a different story of human cultural evolution, the carrier bag theory. One in which the tale of the hero, and how *his* "wonderful" long hard tools for digging, whacking, bashing, grinding, stabbing and cutting have shaped civilisation, is replaced instead by the lesser told story of the container. Le Guin says, "before the tool that forces energy outward, we made the tool that brings energy home"(Le Guin, 1989, 151). Before bringing home the harvest, we first need something to put it in: a sling, a sack, a basket, a net, a trug, a pocket. Perhaps this is a much better story to tell in the face of climate and ecological emergency? One which shifts humanity's story away from narratives celebrating "singular heroes"—be they human or technological—and "domination over nature", to-

2

wards one of gathering, collective action, sharing and interdependence. As feminist scholar Donna Haraway reminds us, "it matters what stories make worlds, what worlds make stories"(Haraway, 2016, 12).

At first glance, it may seem odd for a science fiction writer to have been an influence on a community food growing project. Yet, writers like Le Guin have played an important role in helping us to value the generative potential of storytelling and the power of collective action and shared experience. Stories are relational. They have the power to shift "I" to "we" and to situate our own individual actions within a broader collective project. They can help us to develop a deeper sense of care and responsibility beyond the human, towards those we have begun to call *more-than-human*.[1] The *Town is*

---

1. We adopt the term "more-than-human" in an attempt to address the dominant anthropocentric view of the world and instead revalue the experiences of the multitude of other species, beings, or things (be they alive or supposedly inert) that we share this planet with and are entangled with. After all, humans themselves are made up of entanglements of other beings, e.g. human gut flora. It could be said that humans are already *more-than-human*. A resonant phrase is other-than-human, which attempts to further decentre anthropocentric views.

the Garden team valued the carrier bag story, and others like it, because they complicate oversimplified narratives and point towards other imaginaries, other ways of being. They've helped us, in Le Guin's own words, "imagine some real grounds for hope".[2]

But stories, and storytelling, are not without risk. A story can exist in that tricky space between truth and fiction. They can help us to imagine new ways to live with the earth but they can also reinforce entrenched ideas and beliefs. If the story is good, if the narrative sticks, it can be hard to refute no matter whether it is fictitious or not. As writer and activist George Monbiot argues, "the only thing that can displace a story is a story" (2017, 15). To disrupt an old narrative, to say no to the world it makes, requires not only a refusal of that world and its plot, but the creation of a new story: the plotting of a world to say yes to. This is the action of re-storying: challenging entrenched narratives by paying attention to the stories others tell, those

2. See Ursula K Le Guin's speech accepting the National Book Foundation's Medal for Distinguished Contribution to American Letters at the 65th National Book Awards (November 19, 2014) [video], https://youtu.be/Et9Nf-rsALk

stories most silenced by dominant and dominating voices. We attempted to continuously glance sideways, to other ways of life, to other people's understanding of gardens and environments, as fellow hopefuls, all involved in striving towards a sustainable way of living. This is an ecology otherwise: ecology that looks to the lifeworlds of non-humans, of humans whose knowledges and experiences have been excluded for so long, as well as the ecology of Western scientists.

Throughout the *Town is the Garden* project we let the *story seed the garden*. From this garden, we've been attempting to gather different ways of thinking and doing. Holding them in our baskets, combining, sharing, exchanging, questioning, bartering, gifting. And as one version of the project returns to the humus, we hope that some of the seeds we managed to gather might germinate, that others might yet be gathered and that some might be shared through these chapbooks.

6

Introduction / Storying the development of the Town is the Garden
Joss Allen and Caroline Gatt

In these chapbooks, all sorts of ways of knowing are acknowledged as having been equally central to the process of TiTG, from history of art and queer ecologies, to compost making and seed saving, to anthropological studies of human-plant relations, to foraging and environmental humanities on compost, to artistic interventions in community orchards and many others we did not have space to include.

~Caroline Gatt, this volume

For three years, the *Town is the Garden* team could be found at the margins of the garden. Amongst the weeds and compost heaps, we explored what it might mean to *think with* the garden. Through crafting and caring for gardens, vegetable plots and orchards, we attempted to rethink how Huntly, a small town in the northeast of Scotland, might feed itself as it faces up to the global climate and ecological emergency. Through the processes of learning and sharing skills in relation to growing food, from planting seeds to preserving the harvest, we investigated these moments of collective action as opportunities, to not only learn to feed ourselves, but also to pay better attention to the entanglement of human and more-than-human worlds. We asked: How might the garden be a site of both resistance and resilience? A place for *thinking* and *doing* ecology, otherwise.

And so, with a basket in hand, we followed the garden path to see where it might lead. ...

Town is the Garden began in 2017 with Joss Allen (Green Coordinator), Camille Sineau (Project Assistant) and Lindy Young (Project Gardener), and was joined by Caroline Gatt (Project Assistant) in 2018 and Rhian Davies (Project Assistant) in 2020.

These six chapbooks are an attempt to gather together some of the diverse ways of thinking, doing and knowing that the project explored with some of the people we explored them with.

The Town is the Garden chapbooks

The TiTG chapbooks can be read independently of each other or as a collection but we suggest reading them in this order:

We suggest beginning with *Story I & II*.

In *I*, we source the development of the *Town is the Garden* project through a conversation between the chapbook editors, from the planting of a wood to establishing a seed library, temporarily unearthing the project's roots and surveying the ground around them. In *II*, over four seasons, curator and art historian (and previous Deveron Projects colleague) Elisabetta Rattalino tells us a tale of art and agriculture which begins in a small town outside Rome in 1973, where artist Gianfranco Baruchello begins to plough a field as an artistic experiment. From autumn through winter and spring, we arrive in Huntly in the summer, tracing a journey through a series of artists' works that engage with gardening, growing food and agriculture. Through which Elisabetta tells us that cultivation is an act of caring; one possible path artists have been taking towards dealing with crisis. A path, she suggests, the *Town is the Garden* has also taken. Following our journey through the seasons, we finish with a different story, a *Town is the Garden* fabulation. A poetic version/vision of how our programme unfolded, and a call to get down with the earthworms.

Next, we suggest you read *Compost*.

One of the first things we did as a project was to build a new composting site, and the practice of composting was an important way for us to think through ideas related to care in the ecology of the garden. Here you will find some composting recipes developed from our experiments, alongside an extract from Maria Puig de la Bellacasa's book *Matters of Care: Speculative Ethics in More than*

Human Worlds. We read the chapter "Soil Times" from *Matters of Care* in our very first TiTG reading group, and began a conversation with Maria about coming on a residency in Huntly—it never quite happened but her thinking has been an important influence on us. In the extract included here, "Permaculture practices as ethical doings", through the example of permaculture and specifically the practice of composting, Maria speculates an ethics of care between humans and other-than-humans (e.g. earthworms). This ethics, she suggests, is not based on a strict set of moral principles, but instead based on relationships of interdependency. We have come to think of reading also as a practice of composting: keep returning to it, and *re-turning* it over and over.[3]

Now we have our compost, it is time to turn our attention to *Seeds*.

Dawn Finch is one of the curators, alongside Katrina Flad, of the Strathbogie Seed Collective, an emerging seed library, a seed first sown by the

3. Thank you to Yvonne Billimore through whom we came to this useful term "re-turning" via Karen Barad. See Yvonne Billimore and Jussi Koitela (2020. 26).

Town is the Garden project. In the chapbook *Seeds,* Dawn's text "The seed, the soil and me" teaches us how to save seed, about the beauty of seed saving, and why saving seeds is an important skill to learn. But also that *saving seed is about more than just saving seed.* Learning to save seed, Dawn suggests, is also one possible path towards plant-human intimacy. To save seed is an act of symbiosis. Dawn shares with us two new poems, *Seeds* and *Allotted Time.* We suggest you try to read these aloud with your gardening kin, and why not, again and again: "In the circle of this journey / in this small hard casing / is all the Earth."

After our seeds are sown, we encounter *Plants.*

Exploring the relationship between plants and humans was an important part of the project and we had two teachers to guide us, Eleanor Brown and Alexandra Falter. Eleanor Brown, aka the fermented forager, began working with us right from the very beginning of the project, through an event called *Seasons of Weeds.* Thus, began our journey following and foraging *weedy* plants around Huntly. In "Foraging, an incidental mindfulness prac-

14

tice", Eleanor leads us through her foraging year, introducing us to some of her favourite plants—most of whom, you don't have to look very far to find—and recipes for making the most "of their abundant nutrition and medicine". Eleanor is an advocate of plant *ally-ship* and draws a correlation between caring for our own (gut) health and of the ecosystems that we are a part of. In conversation with Eleanor, she once told us she believes that it is not by chance many of these plants like to grow in close proximity to where humans too have chosen to live. Her text is a gentle call to pay attention to what is growing around you and to the plants you may have overlooked.

Alexander Falter joined us during a workshop to develop a forest garden, where she shared with us some of her research into the relationships between medicinal plants and people. In *Plants,* she shares with us a text called, "Relationships in motion with plants and people in the Bolivian Andes", which reminds us that the relationships between plants and humans are not always "smooth" but instead can often be "disruptive" and even, "problematic". It is a reminder that it doesn't matter where you are, although not universally the same, plants and humans are engaged in relationships of *co-be-*

coming: we are all entangled with the lives of plants and plants with the lives of humans.

Plants grow together to form a *Garden*.

Joe Crowdy joined us in Huntly to help us think about the queering of the garden. We explored the role plants played in fostering human sensuality and intimacy through two workshops, one for the local high school's LQTBQ+ & Allies group— with whom we were planning a garden—and a public one. In the chapbook *Garden*, Joe expands upon these workshops and explores the garden as a site for cultivating queer friendship, a place where the desires of plants and humans meet. Through his text "Cultivating Queer Friendship", we learn about three historic examples of gardens, those of Natalie Barney, Edward Carpenter and Derek Jarman, which have helped cultivate queer intimacy and friendship, in what he calls "a historiography powered by the connecting forces of desire, friendship and vegetal life". Here the garden is not just a backdrop for the cultivation of non-normative forms of intimacy and friendship but a place that "shift[s] our thinking about desire and care, lust and labour". A highly sensuous text, which, should

16

you be able to, we recommend reading within "rosy pink walls of trees and bushes of the garden".[4]

Finally, beyond the borders of our gardens, an *Orchard*.

Orchard is a story about *Future Fruit*. A project with artists Jonathan Baxter and Sarah Gittins, which sought to rethink and reanimate a community orchard, aided by the thinking and insights of Aberdeenshire-born polymath Patrick Geddes. Planted over a decade ago, the orchard had unfortunately become disconnected from the human communities of Huntly and many people living locally knew very little about it. The project was cut short, and so the story of "Future Fruit: Rethinking Huntly from a Geddesian Perspective" is both a description of the project's activities and intentions, centred around an event called *Aeons and Apple Trees,* and a "hospitable critical wager". They

> 4. Included in *Garden* is a recipe for dyeing fabric using copper beech leaves, "Rosy pink walls of trees and bushes of the garden", to create a "beech salon" as described in "Cultivating Queer Friendship" and in which one of Joe's workshops in Huntly took place.

ask, how might we respond to the climate and ecological crisis by learning to care for an orchard?

Storying the development of the Town is the Garden

Throughout the project, questioning and conversation were the modes that characterised how the project team members worked together. For this reason, the description and analysis of the *Town is the Garden* (TiTG) is offered through the same means, a conversation between the two editors of these chapbooks: Joss Allen and Caroline Gatt.

Caroline Gatt (CG): After the very broad overview of the *Town is the Garden* project (TiTG) in the prologue, what I would like to know is what led to the idea of the project?

Joss Allen (JA): It is difficult to trace the roots of *Town is the Garden* and decide exactly when its seeds were sown. But let's begin the story like this: it's March 2015, following a year of planning, over 150 people have gathered to plant a wood just outside Huntly. Many are residents from the surrounding area, from the local school and some have travelled from further afield—including a group of school pupils from Argentina. Together over the course of two days, under the guidance of forester Steve Brown, we plant forty-nine oak trees with a large

(60kg) lump of stone brought from France buried next to each of them. Alongside the oaks, we plant 700 other trees such as silver birch, rowan and hazel, and a thousand shrubs and wildflowers including elder, wood anemone, blackthorn, campion and foxglove. The one and a half hectare wood is being planted as a living monument to peace, as part of a project organised by Deveron Projects and developed with artist Caroline Wendling in response to the centenary of the beginning of the First World War. The project is called *Oaks and Amity.*[5] At the end of the two days we down tools and gather for a group photograph. There is a sense of celebration and achievement; planting trees on this scale has been an incredibly powerful experience. We can see it on each other's faces.

Later that evening I imagine myself buried up to my neck in the forest soil alongside the oak saplings. Soil touching skin. A sweet smell. My body held in suspense, carefully supported within the en-

---

5. The wood was later named *The White Wood*, in relation to white as a colour significant in the discourse surrounding peace and peace movements, and a defining characteristic of many of the trees, shrubs and wildflowers planted, for example white bark (silver birch) or flowers (foxglove). For further information on the project, see Deveron Projects, https://www.deveron-projects.com/white-wood/.

tanglement of partially rotted organic matter, humus, plant roots, mycelia, earthworms, bacteria and other microorganisms that make up the soil. I cannot see them but I feel their touch. I feel my body begin to dissolve until the only thing left is colour. A soil of prismatic hues. The oaks grow—towering above my head. The forest becomes dark. I feel a sense of intimacy and reverence, but also, anxiety. I ask myself, into which future are these trees taking root?

CG: It sounds like the experience had a transformative effect on you.

JA: Yes, still now, the experience of that imagery is palpable. A moment of ecological awareness *and* ecological anxiety, and what I now think of as a sense of *ecological belonging*. The project demanded a shift in my thinking, although it took years afterwards for me to really grasp how planting this wood affected me. It also demanded a shift in the way Deveron Projects as an organisation needed to think and act from then on, in what artists Jonathan Baxter and Sarah Gittins might call, its evolution-involution with/within the town of

21

Huntly.[6]

CG: How did the project shift what had been happening in Deveron Projects?

JA: Since 1995, Deveron Projects has been developing socially-engaged, community-based art projects in the town of Huntly, through a methodological framework known as the "Town is the Venue": foregoing a traditional art space, gallery or venue, projects take place across the town, temporarily occupying, inhabiting, and "activating" various local spaces depending on the particular project, people involved and artist(s) working on it, from empty shops to churches, community centres to pubs—and now a wood.[7] Alongside making projects, Deveron Projects had been attempting to live and promote a sustainable way of life too, for example: growing a small amount of food and composting its food waste in the office garden, promoting walking and other slow modes of

---

6. See Baxter and Gittins (2021, 10).

7. I remember once during a public talk on Deveron Projects while trying to explain their methodology, I instead said *mythology*, the town is the venue mythology. So, for more on Deveron Projects methodology-mythology, see https://www.deveron-projects.com/the-town-is-the-venue/.

transport, buying second-hand furniture for the office, and using recycled unbleached paper for printing. We found that the planting of what is now known as the *White Wood* brought these two strands of its work into a kind of productive conflict: that of developing a people-centred sustainable way of life while working on a short-term project by project basis. In planting the wood, we, as an organisation, had to begin to learn to *think with a forest*—an open-ended, speculative way of thinking, but nonetheless, we had put down roots, both metaphorical and actual. We had a venue to tend to. We had to rethink our ideas around timescales (the lifetime of an oak can be 900 years), support, care, who and what was involved in the production of an artwork or a project like this. Alan Macpherson, a writer and academic who helped plant the wood, described how the planting involved not just the labour of the many human volunteers but "innumerable non-human collaborators" (Macpherson, 2006, 22–31), and would involve many more as the wood developed. For me the project opened up a space to think about peace as a "dynamic engagement with others" including non-human others; to think about a "sociality predicated on peace" where

23

those other-than-humans play a significant role.[8] It made peace an ecological question. For me the wood became more than a symbol of peace; it was also a place for developing a kind of regenerative future thinking, and a place in which to tell alternative *ecological* stories.[9]

This is where the work of artist Joseph Beuys comes in since the project was heavily inspired by him, in particular his project *7000 Oaks* and his idea of social sculpture, an extended conception of art which sought to reaffirm the imaginative *and* transformational power of artistic work. In fact, the oak saplings we planted in Huntly were grown from acorns collected from oak trees planted as part of Beuys's *7000 Oaks* project. Through the *7000 Oaks* project, Beuys

8. See Allen and Zeiske (2010), https://www.deveron-projects.com/site_media/uploads/caroline_wendling_oaks_and_amity_report.pdf.

9. The conversation could have continued here exploring the implications of an arts organisation attempting to think with a forest, particularly in relation to the ambiguous (and ubiquitous) topic of "sustainability" but we will have to cut it short, for now. On the *White Wood* and storytelling, see storyteller and artist Ben Macfadyen and the project *300 Years to Grow*, through which he created a *White Wood Story*, a natureculture story aspiring to still be told 300 years from now, https://www.deveron-projects.com/white-wood-story/.

proposed to reforest Kassel, a city heavily bombed during the Second World War, by planting 7000 oaks trees, part of a wider ambition to make towns and cities "forest-like". For Beuys, the planting of trees was a necessary ecological or "biospheric" action, a way of raising ecological consciousness, and as an "enterprise ... regenerating the life of humankind within the body of society" (Beuys in Cooke, n.d.). For him, the tree was a powerful symbol of regeneration, and planting them, a simple but radical way of proposing one possible, *positive* future for Kassel. In planting the *White Wood*, we too were engaging in an act of regeneration and proposing a possible future for Huntly.

During the period running up to Deveron Projects' own wood planting project, we had become increasingly aware of the impacts of neoliberalism and globalisation on the economy of Huntly. After the arrival of two large supermarkets on the outskirts of town, ten years prior, and a dramatic increase in online shopping, signalling the collapse of traditional retail, many town centre shops and basic amenities had closed. Traditional industries such as farming no longer employed the number of workers they once had and other forms of local employment were becoming increasingly precarious, such as the hospitality sector and oil industry. The economy of the town was suffering. Although not perhaps a direct intervention into the town itself, like Beuys' *7000 Oaks*, through our collective tree planting effort—and my arboreal, *soily* imagining—it became clear to me that these two things, the issues facing Huntly and the planting of a wood, were not separate. The wood wasn't just a place for thinking about ecology (or peace) and the town wasn't just a place for thinking about economy. Thinking with the wood *is* learning to see the relationship between economy and ecology differently, and attempting to re-configure it. Maybe that seems obvious but perhaps I/we needed the kind of ecological imaginary that the wood planting created to see this.

So, the planting of the wood led Deveron Projects to think about the regeneration of the town centre, aided by the thinking of Patrick Geddes, towards developing a five-year programme "New Economies", and ultimately purchasing a town centre property for redevelopment; and me, aided by the thinking of feminist economic geographer JK Gibson-Graham, to rethinking the relationship between ecology and economy (Gibson-Graham and Miller, 2015, 7–16), and how this might be enacted through regenerative forms of agriculture, gardening and food growing.

26

The project *Town is the Garden* was developed from subsequent conversations and questions we had as a team about alternative economies, food (we were always thinking about food) and the role of gardening in town regeneration. Could we host a "gardener in residence", as we did with artists? What does it mean to "green" the town centre? Could we guerrilla garden an orchard or a meadow in the town square? Could we rethink the local food economy from the ground up?

In sum, planting trees as a symbol of peace and regeneration led to the idea of exploring gardening as an ecologically regenerative practice and the development of the *Town is the Garden* project. I think it is important to trace the lineage of its development, particularly because these stories can often be left out from the wider, singular narrative or curatorial strategy that an arts organisation might choose to make public. These are the kind of entangled backstories I like to hear and think with.

I'd like to hear your backstory, your roots before joining the TiTG team in June 2018. Coming from an academic career in anthropology, how did you come to be involved in the TiTG project? Why the change from teaching and research to growing food?

27

CG: In 2016 I was returning to my research position at the University of Aberdeen after an extended period of sick leave followed by a year's maternity leave. It was a challenging time and I was lucky to have had lots of support including from occupational health, coaches and my GP. It was also a rather turbulent time in broader world politics. It was the year of the Brexit referendum, Trump won the USA presidential elections, environmental crises from floods to uncontrollable forest fires carried on around the world even though not given much attention in British media. It felt to me that we were nearing an almost apocalyptic period where political situations would soon combine with environmental ones to threaten the safety of my life and the life of my family. One night I dreamt that me, my husband and our daughter, then one year old, were being herded into enclosures and at one shocking moment, we were forced to separate: the women in one group, the men in another and the children alone in a separate group. The terror of that holocaust-informed dream haunts me to this moment, to the extent I was afraid to begin typing it. When I awoke, shaking, terrified, with deep dread aching in my whole body, I began imagining scenarios we all know too well from recent human histo-

28

ry where totalitarian political movements combine with actual or threatened deprivation to cause monumental global tragedies such as the Second World War. I projected scenarios of which nations would be a threat, where would the terror zones possibly be in terms of conflict or ghettoisation, where would there be the most space and resources that could accommodate refugees; have enough water, where could I take my family to hide and survive what I was sure was coming. I became convinced I needed to learn how to grow food and that my dependence on the Internet for knowledge on providing the basics for life was short-sighted: there would be no Internet in my imagined apocalypse.

JA: That is a really distressing scenario. Thank you for sharing, it can't have been easy.

CG: You're right, the personal story I share above may be uncomfortable, even painful for you and others to read. It was certainly painful to remember and write. However, this was an example of what Donna Haraway has identified as a type of futurism, a "game over" response to the current environmental and social catastrophes based on apocalyptic visions of the future (2016, 3) (even if in my imaginings this terrifying future was not very far off). Here was my despair, and it was paralysing. For this reason, Haraway argues that instead of any futurism, either one based on despair or on hope, which in her understanding of hope leads to inaction of other sorts, in order to act and live response-ably on a damaged earth we need to "stay with the trouble", the title of her book.[10] Staying with the trouble entails developing a particular kind of attention to the present, one which may seem familiar to those who practice mindfulness but which actually invites us to loosen the grip of our certainties. Haraway's thick, sensuous attention to the present calls us to attend to constitutive relations everywhere; around us, through us, are us. She draws on natural history and biological studies to show how everything is made through sympoeisis,

10. Not all understandings of hope imply inaction. In fact, in Miyazaki's (2004) ethnography of how Suvavou people, Fiji, work towards compensation for the loss of their ancestral lands, hope is what enables his interlocutors to carrying on working for this compensation in the face of repeated rejection. In this ethnography hope keeps future possibilities open and therefore justifies continued action. The hope Haraway refers to, is a hope of being "saved" from environmental collapse either by some technological or God-sent fixes which entail that no major transformations are required in our daily ways of life (Haraway, 2016, 3).

a making-with. Thinking about individuals, whether individual humans or individual species is no longer viable. The presentism Haraway advocates is replete with inheritances and remembering, and full of "comings, of nurturing what might still be" (ibid 2), but where our certainties need stirring up. She pleads, we will need to attend to multi-species justice, to "make kin as oddkin rather than, or at least in addition to, godkin and genealogical and biogenetic family" (Ibid., 2), and overall it "matters what stories we tell to tell other stories with".

The catastrophic thinking I experienced was diagnosed as situational anxiety, and with support and medication sleep returned and panic subsided. However, what emerged from it was a conviction that learning how to grow food was an essential skill that I needed to learn. This led me in 2018, at the end of my fixed-term research position, to apply for a job as project assistant in a growing project in the small rural town of Huntly, thirty miles west of Aberdeen. I had heard of Deveron Projects from Camille Sineau, an architect who was doing his Masters in Anthropology at Aberdeen, who I knew fairly well. He had joined Deveron Projects to work on this garden project and although I didn't understand much about the project or what his work on it was, it inspired me and offered a way to learn how to grow food, or so I thought. So when I was selected for the position I was thrilled and after long discussions with my husband, we decided to take up the one year job and move the family to Huntly.

What I found myself involved in was a food growing project, yes, and now some years later I find I have the confidence to grow vegetables from seed, enough that during the lockdown in 2020 I grew a good portion of the vegetables my family ate that year. However, I also found myself involved in what Haraway (2016) would call tentacular thinking. I found myself being enabled to explore how to open up possibilities for making relations. The anthropology work I had been doing with Friends of the Earth International (Gatt, 2018) and with laboratory theatre practitioners (Gatt, 2017, 2018) was welcomed and encouraged by you, Joss. In this project I found the opening for understanding those relations Haraway refers to as oddkin, and the possibility to nurture them: relations with the many participants in the *Town is the Garden*, including human colleagues, and other Huntly residents, but also with the plants we were getting to know, the worms and microorganisms in soil, in our gut, on our skin, stones in the vegetable plots, granite buildings and asphalt pavements, rain water, chloramine in tap water that prevented my vegetables from fermenting, wood and linseed oil, sheet plastic and cardboard …

JA: … And old carpets! So far, we've discussed the roots of the TiTG project in the context of the work of Deveron Projects, an organisation that positions itself as a socially engaged arts organisation, from my perspective as involved in the work of DP and as an art worker myself. And you've explained your reasons for joining the project. However, as an anthropologist who has carried out research on environmentalism and the performative arts, how do you position the project in relation to art? Whereabouts in the project do you see art?[11] A question we were always being asked both from within DP and externally.

CG: During my very first day of work, after having visited Deveron Projects several times, I was invited to participate in a meeting with the funding officers from Creative Scotland. As part of this meeting you

11. Thanks to Elisabetta Ratallino for some of the questions, including this one, as well as suggesting to us the structure of an interview which we developed into a conversation.

and Lindy took us around town visiting only some of the various sites where the *Town is the Garden* project had ongoing work: the Brander Garden, wooden planters replete with edible plants offered to local businesses along a central road and the Huntly Square, the allotment. What jumped to mind participating in the conversations with Creative Scotland that day was how was TiTG an art project, or even a socially-engaged art project? Exactly this question that you're asking, where was the art? Of course, this is a question that Creative Scotland were asking. You had explained that it was also a question you and Elisabetta Ratallino asked in the development of the funding applications for TITG during her time at Deveron Projects as Art and Community Worker (2016–17). In fact, this is a question that has been central in the philosophy of art at least since the 1990s (Gell, 1995, 15), and arguably has been ever since the shift towards conceptual art at the turn of the 20th century (Ibid.).

As I got to know the people working at DP and how they related to the project there seemed to be at least two different understandings of where the art was in this project. One understanding was that the elements of design that different members brought to the project was considered by some to mark it out as

34

an artists' gardening project, in comparison to many other gardening projects that didn't attend to their aesthetic in the same way. Another view was that the perceptual skills artists develop, including not taking things at face value, routinely asking questions of the processes, materials and engagements of the work, challenging assumptions and so on, made this an art project in its approach.

The second view situates TiTG in what is referred to as the social turn in contemporary art (Bishop, 2006; Sansi, 2015). Since the late 90s and early noughties, artists began referring to their work as "social practice" (Ibid.). Sansi (Ibid., 2) writes that these artists

> were less interested in art as a form of self-expression than in working in public spaces and on specific sites, developing research with social groups, and addressing questions of immediate political relevance. In other words, they were almost like anthropologists; some of them even had a university degree in Anthropology! Many of them said that they were not actually interested in 'art' itself, but in the things one can do with art.

One of the projects Sansi describes in his introduction resonates closely with TiTG. The project *inside-out: Jardí del Cambalache* "Garden of Barter" (2001) was run by artist Federico Guzmán together with curator Rosa Pera. For this project, they built a network of reciprocity in a contemporary art museum in Barcelona. The project was based on ethnographic research on and with *colonos* ("colonists"), who were mostly rural immigrants to Barcelona who occupied abandoned plots of land on the periphery of the city and turned them into gardens. One of the *colonos* involved in the study offered the vegetables he cultivated to the public in exchange for any item they liked. The project included other activities such as an exhibit on the use of plants, workshops on how to create urban gardens, and an international conference, including the anthropologist Michael Taussig and a final picnic. Unaware of the *Jardí del Cambalache* project, TiTG included all these sorts of activities: workshops, meals, reading groups, public talks/conferences (TiTG invited the anthropologist Cristina Grasseni, Principal Investigator in the European Research Council project called "Food citizens? Collective food procurement in European cities: solidarity and diversity, skills and scale"), people's assemblies, the Barter Shop, community growing projects and events, and many other activities.

Rather than being based on an ethnography of a particular group though, TiTG, in resonance with developments in social theory (see Bryant, Srnicek, Harman, 2011), was a speculative exploration of the relationship between food, from growing food to cooking, preserving and economic systems of exchange, and the current social and environmental catastrophes the world is currently facing. In addition, having just completed a five-year project on collaborative processes, I was acutely aware of Hal Foster's (1995) critique of the ethnographic turn in the arts. The interest and use of ethnography in artists' projects, in Fosters' critique tended to objectify, simplify or even misrepresent the peoples artists were carrying out "ethnography" with. The approach we took in TiTG was more along the lines of offering "provotypes" (Donovan and Gunn, 2012): we offered things aimed at stimulating discussion and exchange. The activities we organised were offered as much as possible for "free", though it is important to be aware that gift-giving is neither necessarily equitable nor freely given. Sansi (2013, 71) notes how anthropologists have long shown that exchanges of gifts can be hierarchical and generate obligations. Further, through these gift exchanges it is possible to form not only social relations, but the very beings we are.

Sansi (Ibid.) makes the connection between these developments in anthropology and the social turn in contemporary art especially in relation to Nicolas Bourriaud's (2002) *Relational Aesthetics*. For Bourriaud, relational art works produce models of sociality that aim to intervene in social and political realities (2002, cited in Sansi, 2015, 11). In other words, relational art works "propose a kind of experimental laboratory of the minimal elements of everyday life, the basic forms of social relation, like an act of gift-giving, with all its ambiguity, by putting them into play in unexpected ways" (Sansi, 2015, 12).

JA: Interesting that you make reference to relational aesthetics but I think I would be wary of mentioning it without drawing attention to some of its problems. Particularly, for example, that many of these works are still highly choreographed and presented in such a way that maintains a certain kind of division between the artist(s) and the audience or those "experiencing" the work. In this sense, the projects Bourriaud refers to seem less interested in actually examining or calling into question these new or different ways of producing intersubjective or social relations than with how these "scenarios" or "models of sociality" are displayed.[12]

CG: In fact, what was actually most important for us in TiTG was precisely questioning those relations, and the ways we narrate them, or how they can be traced in what we grow, cook and eat. In addition, we attempted to be aware of the relations of power and obligation that gifting entailed. One issue that we were very aware of was the fact that many of the participants in our activities seemed to share very similar views to ours. We were concerned that the project would turn out to be an echo chamber. Not everyone accepted the gifts we offered. However, after a number of failed attempts to organise events in places and contexts that we thought may be accessible to "different" understandings, we decided that actually to support those in Huntly attempting to develop what we could consider "ecological" ways of life was a valid effort.

JA: So, supporting and developing critical local efforts at sustainability was the "art" of TiTG?

CG: Actually, what I think is essential here, is that

12. This is part of a long-standing debate in socially engaged art, see Bishop (2004, 51–79); and Kester (2011).

asking where the art is *cannot be the question*, it must be the object of our questioning. Neither art, nor for that matter anthropology, can or should retain its current distinction in the light of the role each of these spheres play in the very system that has led to the current global social and environmental crises. Very broadly art, anthropology and all other western disciplines are based on the very same historical foundations as the system that separates nature from culture. This system functions along the same cultural logic that relegates non-Western understandings of the world to mere "belief", which is in turn part of the deep tragedy of colonial pasts and presents. More specifically, art as a separate discipline / practice / sphere within this system, identifies creativity as innovation, rather than creativity as improvisation (Ingold and Hallam, 2007). The effect of this understanding of creativity as rupture is that the figure of the artist is actually a key persona of capitolo-modernity: the artist as genius making a break with tradition. The approach a number of anthropologists are taking to counter this is anti-disciplinary (Sansi, 2015, 16).[13] However, what this entails is not a lack of recogni-

13. See also Ingold et al, *Knowing From the Inside*, https://www.abdn.ac.uk/research/kfi/about/.

tion for how different practices and ways of knowing emerge from communities and lineages of knowledge and skill. Rather being anti-disciplinary here entails acknowledging that any discipline was always already heterogenous, and included all sorts of sources of knowledge and ways of knowing and practices that are not acknowledged in strict disciplinary definitions. Being anti-disciplinary is also a call to recognising the ongoing negotiation that forms any way of knowing (Ang and Gatt, 2018). In fact, being anti-disciplinary is an essential way to acknowledge those ways of knowing that have been routinely excluded as not being "properly academic", such as Indigenous ways of knowing, performative ways of knowing, neurodiverse ways of knowing and so on, that have actually participated in shaping modern disciplines such as "art" and "anthropology" (Gatt, 2022; Safier, 2010). In these chapbooks, all sorts of ways of knowing are acknowledged as having been equally central to the process of TiTG, from history of art and queer ecologies, to compost making and seed saving, to anthropological studies of human-plant relations, to foraging and environmental humanities on compost, to artistic interventions in community orchards and many others we did not have space to include.

JA: Yes, and the role of story as well, as an important way of producing and sharing knowledge.

CG: So, we've discussed how the project sits in relation to the art world, and I am sure we could continue this further, but TiTG wasn't funded by an art fund, was it? So how did you then go on to develop the actual project as a result of your experiences with the White Wood?

JA: So, the idea developed into a project supported by the Climate Challenge Fund (CCF), a Scottish Government initiative to support community-led organisations to reduce local carbon emissions. It is important to mention the fund here because the CCF—its aims and objectives—ultimately influenced the direction and development of the project. In line with the fund, we would support the communities of Huntly to reduce their carbon emissions through gardening, primarily through growing more of their own food, changing their food eating habits (to be more seasonal, less wasteful) and composting more of their own food waste locally. Learning about growing food, we agreed, was a good thing. Reducing carbon emissions was a good thing: an achievable, measurable, *quantifiable* way to tackle climate

42

change. So, the project began in spring 2017 with Lindy Young as the project gardener, Camille Sineau as the project assistant and myself as the green coordinator (project coordinator)—being also tasked with dealing with Deveron Projects environmental reporting and policy writing. We set about developing a programme and strategy for engaging people in the project.

We would have to report to our funders quarterly with data that could be used to calculate the carbon emission reductions the project had helped generate locally. This involved asking participants involved in the project to weigh the produce they had grown, to weigh the amount of food/garden waste they had composted (that would have otherwise gone to landfill) and to record how their knowledge and behaviour had changed after attending any of our events. The data collection was fairly laborious but we felt it was worth it and valuable, a barometer of our collective effort in reducing carbon emissions. It made sense to us: that reducing carbon emissions was an important part of the work of regeneration; that the project needed something to measure its success and failures by. In the rush of the first couple of months to get going there wasn't much time for critical reflection, to catch the season we had to get going/growing *quickly*. And yet there were a number of questions we kept returning to—the grit in our shoes, the dirt under our fingernails.

Firstly, why should we all grow our own food? We questioned whether it was fair to assume that everyone in Huntly was in a position to do this? Who had access to the necessary resources, whether that be time, money or land? We questioned what kind of narrative this might play into? Could this "grow your own" directive also be acting as a mask for the shifting of responsibility for dealing with a poorly distributed and unjust food system, and more broadly the climate and ecological emergency, onto communities and individuals rather than taking measures at corporate, national and systemic levels? Especially without enabling those individuals with time and resources actually needed to grow their own.

Secondly, who gets to decide what a sustainable future looks like? Again, we questioned what kinds of stories were being told here. The scale and implications of the climate and ecological emergency are pretty difficult to grasp, to understand the causes and likely effects, and your potential complicity in it all. Emphasising the importance of individual actions, however, without trying to identify and address some really fundamental questions and ideas upon which

44

industrialised society is premised, seemed like turning a hugely complex problem into one which could seemingly be fixed through consumer activism, objective metrics and techno-fixes, effectively through *greening* capitalism.

We began to see flaws in running a project so heavily focused on metrics and data collection. For example, if one participant grows only potatoes for a year, and another grows only lettuce, who has done more to address climate change? The carbon metrics would say the former—potatoes weighing significantly more than lettuce. But those lettuces might have taught you more about your place within an ecological community than growing kilos of potatoes. If we focus too heavily on counting our carbon emissions are we failing to deal with the complexities and intersectionality of the problem? More importantly, what kind of world are we collectively imagining through counting carbon emissions, through imposing a single measure of value on what sustainability looks like? It isn't a particularly appealing vision, and one thoroughly embedded within a neoliberal and capitalist agenda, which I think is irreconcilable with the idea of an *ecologically* sustainable future. What we need as Michael Mikulak says are "compelling narratives that simultaneously challenge the system and provide alternatives" (2013, 37). These metrics seem to play into a narrative which does neither, rather, one which has already been foreclosed within the limits of a consumerist future where it is still the growth of the economy above all else: "Cut your carbon emissions so we can keep the economy growing." To borrow a line from Ursula K. Le Guin's *The Lathe of Heaven*, perhaps such an approach would "not change anything radically; only quantifiably" (2018, 44).

So, how else could we view this? We asked, what do alternative food growing movements have to offer? It is quite easy to get carried away by the heady, sanguine movement around growing food. That harks back to the land, reconnecting with nature, self-sufficient, sustainable "good life" vibe is appealing—for many important and admirable reasons. Growing food can be very empowering; it can totally change your outlook on life. I think we need to nurture a sense of hope and optimism in these uncertain times, and learning to grow your own food is certainly one possible path towards doing this. Anyone who has ever sown a seed is aware of this; to sow a seed is to practice being hopeful for the future. It is an inherently optimistic act, and this filters through the whole experience of growing food. As Dawn Finch mentions in her text on seed saving, it is also a way to develop a deeply personal relationship with plants, soil and season, with things other-than-human—this sense of ecological awareness I mentioned earlier. There is something powerful about engaging in the food growing movement, and its ability to capture many peoples' collective imagination shouldn't be dismissed, but it is not without its problems either.

We were wary of uncritically celebrating the "grow your own" movement and the alternative food practices associated with it. A wide field of practices and practitioners, growers, activists, producers, farmers'-market-goers and "foodies", who can often be hugely varied and contradictory (contradiction not necessarily being a bad thing) bunch in their values and approaches, that can feel exclusive and inaccessible to many (in terms of both linguistic and economic terms), and whose exponents are often associated with certain class backgrounds or gendered relationships with food—this is of course not the same globally or historically. It/they can draw heavily on narratives that hark back to "those halcyon days" and some past relationship between humans and the land; a tendency to idealise a kind of relationship which might not have really existed, or at

47

least not without its own set of problems.[14] This is certainly something you and I have discussed before when words like "reconnect" kept slipping into the description of the project or copy for events. There can also be a tendency to gloss everything over with a thick emulsion of hopefulness and optimism, without perhaps giving space to think about some of the trickier and more difficult work that also needs to be done. To deal with ecological anxiety—like I felt after planting the wood or that you experienced after returning to Aberdeen University.

I think though, through asking these questions, I became quite aware of how tricky and ambiguous the word "sustainable" is, particularly when preceding nouns like "development" or "growth". Sustainable is derived from sustain—"to give support to", "to endure without failing", "to suffer". I wasn't entirely convinced about the kind of sustainable future this project was giving root to. A neoliberal, capitalist future was not something I personally wanted to support or to endure.

So, these questions really shaped how the project developed in the first few months. We still asked

14. For more on the rich history of gardening and food growing in the UK, see Willes (2014); and Crouch and Ward (1997).

48

participants to weigh their food and count carbon emissions; we were still interested in rethinking how a community like Huntly might feed itself, and that growing more food locally at home, in peoples' gardens and in public could be part of this, but we also tried to avoid being too prescriptive. I think we were quite honest about not knowing what a sustainable future looked like, and that we were trying to figure that out through learning about food growing. In this sense, the idea of "provotyping", you mentioned earlier, seems apt. I think we were cautious of seeing the project as some kind of ameliorative effort. We saw it more as a way to share and develop communal knowledge while also trying to make the complex sensible, and not just through data gathering or theory, but in a way where creative practices could play more than an illustrative role in this.

The project really became about, how could we deal with these questions, and others, through learning to grow food together? To explore the entanglement of human lives with those other-than-humans, relationships of interdependence and of exploitation, what nature and culture are and their apparent separation. The garden seemed like a really productive place to explore these questions and tensions, as well as for sharing and producing communal knowledge.

As a site of both resistance and resilience; a place from which to make a stand against an ecologically unsustainable future with the plants and creatures of the garden; and a place to rebound back from a path heading towards climate and ecological emergency, towards *whatever is emerging*.

CG: Yes we thought a lot about how to work with ecology otherwise.

JA: Exactly, and I was/have been really influenced by the writing of Robin Wall Kimmerer, she says, "a garden is a nursery for nurturing connection, the soil for cultivation of practical reverence" (Kimmerer, 2013). I really agree with this. I think we wanted to nurture that sense of ecological awareness that gardening can create, that sense of joy and hopefulness but also not to avoid dealing with the problematic ecological relations that are also found in the garden, where humans often attempt to exert a sense of domination and control over nature, where they dig rows and create borders, and weed out the kinds of things they don't want to see. How could we think and do ecology differently with the garden?

CG: Yes in fact there is a long history of gardening for more than just subsistence purposes, or at least that gardens have always been aesthetic and cultural as well as for subsistence.[15] In fact three of the chapbooks include a discussion of some of these different histories. Elisabetta Rattalino in this chapbook explores the history of artworks by means of agriculture, Joe Crowdy explores a queer history of the garden, and Alexander Falter, the changing relationship between people and plants in the Bolivian Andes. Gardening is imbued in so many ways with those stories we discussed earlier, stories that compose us and stories for shifting narratives with.

JA: TiTG then was one aesthetic and cultural gardening project amongst many others. The context of TiTG, run in Huntly with its particular market town history meant that on reflection the TiTG gardening story came into conversation with the stories already being told in the area. Do you think the rural character of the area, and the particular gardening cultures in Huntly, affected the project?

CG: It certainly did! Here's some context: Huntly

15. Thanks to Jo Vergunst for reminding us of this.

is a small market town in the northeast of Scotland, thirty miles west of Aberdeen. It has a population of circa 4800, many of whom are retired agriculturalists, though I couldn't get my hands on precise statistics on previous employment. Aberdeenshire, especially the area surrounding Huntly has been characterised by large scale farms, typically covering larger areas than the average farms in mainland Europe. Cereals, general cropping, including potatoes and barley (mostly for the whisky industry), cattle rearing and sheep rearing dominate the agricultural landscape and have done since the mid 1800s. Although in the last handful of decades these farms have been increasingly mechanised, a good majority of the town's inhabitants' lives were formed in relation to this agricultural history. Reminiscing about harvesting potatoes during the annual "Tattie holidays" in October dominates discussions on two Facebook groups "Huntly Histories" and "Huntly Toon Blether" (Huntly Town Chat), each group having more than 5000 members. During the Tattie Holidays, all schools in the area are shut and up until the 70s at least, children would join their parents and families harvesting potatoes for these two weeks. However, the number of people currently working on farms today has dropped radically, with some statistics citing insignificant numbers currently employed in agriculture.[16]

An interesting anomaly in Huntly (according to many people I engaged with) is the well-known presence, locally, nationally and internationally, of Deveron Projects (DP), an organisation that defines itself as a "socially engaged arts organisation". DP was founded in 1995 by Claudia Zeiske who came to live in Huntly with her family. While the demographic trend in Huntly is for outward migration, especially of young adults, a steady stream of people come to work at DP from all over the world each year. People come to work as interns who come for an average three-month stay, invited artists, who until recently also came for three-month stays. Now, however, projects last longer, up to two years, but the artist might only stay for up to ten days. Finally, a few, like yourself, who worked for DP for 6 years, and myself, come to DP to work as employees for somewhat longer periods.

JA: Yes, although some others have returned for various stints.

CG: Talking to people in Huntly over the three

16. See https://www.usp.scot/.

53

years that I have lived here, it is clear that DP divides opinions between those who value its presence and activities as enriching, and those who find that DP embodies and perpetuates socio-economic divisions that classically surround the "art world". A considerable amount of friction arises from xenophobic attitudes towards the fact that the founder, Zeiske, and most of the people who come to work with DP are not native to Huntly. This is sometimes explicit, even if not acknowledged as xenophobia. Most often dislike of DP is framed in terms of personal relations, people feeling snubbed. In debates around what is considered art, the discussion of being snubbed becomes more complex in relation to the prolific community of crafters in the North East. Some of these crafters also frame their relationship with DP in terms of feeling snubbed, certainly not all of them. There is no space to go into this discussion here, although an ethnography of Deveron Projects would provide much-needed insights into questions of belonging, community building, as well as the role of the arts, in a post-Brexit Scotland. What is important for this introduction is to note the energy Huntly residents invest in the friction surrounding DP and that TiTG was set up in the context of this long-standing friction.

A little more information about Huntly will also be important. There is a clear distinction between town and countryside. This is a common feature across agricultural societies in Europe and the Mediterranean, where creating clear categories of separation has been interpreted as being part of agriculturalists identity formation as carers and nurturers of an otherwise unruly "Nature".[17]

Although many houses and public buildings have garden areas, virtually none of these are used to grow edible plants anymore, though they were in the past. In the rarer instances where vegetables and fruit are grown these are most commonly not grown in the "front garden". Most front gardens are dominated by grass, gravel, paving, flowers and ornamental plants, sometimes in the ground, sometimes in pots atop paved or gravelled ground. Currently, Huntly Square has no permanent planting areas, although until the 1980s there were large trees and spacious beds all around the square. Nowadays, every spring the Aberdeenshire Council in collaboration with a local Rotary Club place large black plastic planters around the square, overflowing with colourful and

17. See, for instance, Theodoussopoulos (2003); Gruppuso (2018); Silverman (1975).

lush annual plants and flowers. Most of these are imported from mainland Europe as mature or young plants. Most are F1 hybrids and offer little in the way of forage for bees and insects.[18] All are discarded at the end of autumn. The imaginary and concomitant aesthetic that I encountered when I joined the *Town is the Garden* project was significantly different to the dominant understanding of "Nature" in Huntly residents' gardens.

JA: Could you elaborate?

CG: One of the activities of TiTG that I was in-

18. "F1 hybrid" is the term used for the first generation hybrid seed/plant that occurs following the successful cross-pollination of one genetically uniform plant variety with another specific genetically uniform variety. The first generation of a hybridised plant cross also tends to grow better and produce higher yields than the parent varieties due to a phenomenon called "hybrid vigour". However, any seed produced by F1 plants is genetically unstable and cannot be saved for use in following years. So if buying F1 plants, new seed needs to be bought every year. In addition the only way to make F1 hybrids economically viable, since human-made hybrids are done by targeted pollination rather than open pollination, is to use Cytoplasmic Male Sterility (CMS), which means that the plants are unable to produce their own pollen.

troduced to in my first few days of work were the edible planters dotted around the square and main two streets. These were handmade, unpainted but treated wooden planters, planted only with hardy edible perennial plants. They included a wide variety of herbs, flowers and medicinal plants such as different varieties of mint, thyme, oyster plant, sage, feverfew, dwarf juniper … Some of the larger planters included squashes with plump yellow fruit. All plants were sourced from an organic nursery some 75 miles north on the Black Isle. These planters had been made by the TiTG team and offered to local businesses, and were intended to be there indefinitely, surviving with minimal care through all the seasons. Not everything went as planned with these planters. First of all, most of the businesses did not care for the planters, and the summer of 2019 having been a considerably drier summer than was usual meant that a good number of the plants died, needed replacing or simply didn't look as appealing as when they were first planted. The planters were placed directly on the pavement and were only circa 30cm tall, at most 60cm tall. This meant that dogs fowled them and salt from gritters got into them. Both dog urine and grit killed many of the plants, but this also meant that none of the plants were actually suitable for tasting and smelling

57

as had been hoped for by TiTG. Finally, wild plants also managed to grow alongside the ones TiTG had planted. In late autumn 2019, by which time I was now an integral member of the team, TiTG had also placed six apple trees in similar handmade wooden planters all around the square. These also had mints and self-seeded wild plants growing around the base of the apple trees.

At the time DP had been approached by members of the Rotary Club, who managed the black flower planters, complaining that the wooden planters around the square were not well maintained, didn't match with the aesthetic of the Square, did not have enough flowers in them and were mainly planted with "weeds". This dislike for weeds in the town's main roads and public spaces, such as the Square is a view shared by a large number of Huntly residents. For instance, during the quiet summer of 2020, throughout the first lockdown in Scotland, I was still tasked with caring for the remaining apple trees and other perennials in wooden planters in Huntly Square and Deveron Street. That summer, wild plants such as poppies, ivy-leaved toadflax, purple toadflax, white stonecrop (sedum album), dandelions of course, even some sort of brassica and grasses managed to flourish all along the pavement and building edges. These wild plants managed to grow because the Aberdeen-shire Council, who would otherwise routinely spray weed killer along the edges of all the pavements, had stopped all but essential services during the lock-down. However, every morning I could hear a distinct and loud scraping echoing through the empty streets. This was the sound of a Dutch hoe being passionately applied to the removal of weeds along the town's main streets. This Dutch hoe belonged to a retired man, who every day, almost without exception, removed as much of the wild plants growing in the pavement and road cracks along the streets of Huntly as he could. He was highly praised for this work by many members of the Huntly Toon Blether, who repeatedly celebrated his efforts throughout summer for keeping the town "clean".

What is evident in the Rotary's complaints about the weeds in the wooden planters and in the celebrated daily work of the elderly gentleman and his Dutch hoe is a particular urban ideal. Through an arduous struggle, European towns and cities took on a particular quality in the 19th Century: streets were turned from muddy, wet and odorous to the "abiotic" city, where soils and anything growing in them from diseases to plants and animals, were sealed over with asphalt, and liquids of all sorts channelled out of sight and smell (Meulemans, 2017). Although the TiTG project successfully spoke to many local residents' imaginary of the whole of Huntly being a lush garden, *which* plants were welcome in that garden and importantly *where* those plants were welcome to live brought to the fore diverging understandings of "Nature" and of the "Town".

On the one hand, a mainstream understanding of a garden and a town in Huntly engages in hard work to keep certain categories separate. On the other, the TiTG team explored and celebrated wild plants and weeds (see chapbook *Plants*). Rather than considering wild plants as being out of place, messy, or dirty, you and I see these as forms of resistance, I believe, correct me if you disagree. These are the silent hopefuls that will find ways of living in the ruins of capitalism.

JA: Yes absolutely! Co-conspirators for flourishing in the ruins!

CG: In fact, the abiotic town can soon become a garden; abundant in life and food for humans and other creatures, if we are prepared to challenge our assumptions. The friction also lay in the argument that these daily assumptions in 21st Century Scotland, those aesthetic and moral principles embedded in an "abiotic" urban ideal are intimately entwined with modernity and capitalism, world systems that have led to the current environmental and social catastrophe (Tsing et al, 2016). I'm sure you can see me struggling between the supposedly empathetic voice of the social scientist and the impassioned voice of the disagreement I felt with many Huntly residents about things like weed killer.

Beyond this disparity in narratives of nature, an unexpected outcome of the TiTG project was that people who had otherwise not been keen on DP for one reason or another were in fact interested in participating in gardening activities. To return to our earlier conversation about art, many people participated in the TiTG project precisely because it seemed to sit *outside* of the world of "art". What this enabled was that the different participants brought to the TiTG project their skills, and the communities of practice they were part of. This included artists and gardeners, small farmers, crafters, cooks and many others. Essentially, the TiTG project became a nexus for multiple practices and histories, in which art was only one thread. In this sense, the particular character of Huntly certainly did shape the project, because the specific experiences and practices of those who participated in it shaped it. For this reason, this edited collection brings together some of these different threads and binds them together in the sorts of conversations that happened through the TiTG project.

CG: Finally, TiTG didn't receive follow-on funding from the CCF. Has the project ended or does it live on in some other forms? How was TiTG sustainable itself?

JA: So yes, in many ways the project came to a close at the end of March 2020, it returned to the compost heap so to speak. As the project itself decomposed, some things were left behind (a publicly available resource library and archive, and a community orchard) and some other forms emerged (a climate action group, a garden for the local high school LGBTQ+ group and a seed library). I'll mention a couple of those shortly, but first I would like to just briefly discuss the idea of sustainability a little further—although it really demands a much longer discussion. Towards the end of the project, I felt there was a lot of pressure to make the project financially sustainable beyond the CCF funding, and to continue to deliver some kind of programme and for the

62

community support to not just suddenly disappear. This is a problem, particularly within the arts, where projects are so dependent on what is often very short-term funding that to think longer-term can be really challenging. These funding rhythms can be quite disruptive, where sometimes it feels like you've only just got started and then suddenly you have to shift your focus and energy towards reporting, trying to apply for more funding, or for looking for another job. We were lucky to get three years. So, one critique made against the project was that for a project perceived to be dealing with sustainability to not become sustainable beyond grant funding dependency was a failure. A critique I've wrestled with since the project finished. There were other options we could have tried to make the continuation sustainable, such as applying to other funds, charging people to attend workshops, selling produce or some kind of service. But to give a very honest answer, I felt the project had run its course. It was no longer sustainable for me because I no longer had the energy to sustain it—and I think neither did the rest of the team (both TiTG and DP). For my own well-being, I had to move on. Questions of wellbeing and care are so often missed out from conversations about sustainability. Instead, I find the focus is predominantly on growth and development and on keeping things going, which is often rooted in a very un-diverse understanding of economy, in which to be sustainable really only means to be financially sustainable.

For me decomposition is also a really important process in any discussion on sustainability—the compost heap taught us that. As the project began composting, we hoped we would be leaving behind fertile ground for other things to grow, and we made plans to support some of these growths and transitions. DP had already begun another project looking at food, the *Neep & Okra Kitchen*, and whose project team shared many similar ideas and ambitions as our own, particularly about exploring more ecological ways of being through food and food growing. So, we collaborated on a number of events as a way to transition and make space for them.[19]

19. This included film screenings, meals and gardening workshops. One event in particular, *GRAFT*, organised with Jonathan Baxter and Sarah Gittins, was intended to make this transition public, see https://www.deveron-projects.com/events/graft/. And our final weekend of events, *Seeds and Saplings*, was a collaboration with the Neep & Okra team based around the Perisian tradition of Nowruz, which included the launching of the Strathbogie Seed Collective, an orchard care and maintenance session, planting apple trees, and an evening celebratory meal and film screening of Jumana Manna's *Wild Relatives* (2018), see

Unfortunately, as readers will discover in *Orchard*, one of our intended seedlings, to help reanimate a local community orchard that had become neglected (by humans), failed to mature. Originally planned as a two-year project with artists Jonathan Baxter and Sarah Gittins, reaching beyond the ending of the TiTG CCF funding, the project had to be cut short as Deveron Projects felt it wasn't a priority for them while they focused on the redevelopment of a town centre property and change in leadership. This was understandable but also hugely disappointing as we (the TiTG team and Jonathan and Sarah) had viewed this as a really important community site, especially as a place for continuing to think and do ecology otherwise. We were interested in the orchard as a multi-species commons through which we could explore ideas of kinship, care and interdependence, and of course celebrate the gift of fruit. After TiTG finished, there were many difficult months trying to find a way forward for the orchard, as institutional support disappeared, and as various different people, ideas, desires, actions and energies collided, before a possible solution emerged. I remained involved, albeit from my new Helsinki home, supporting the

https://www.deveron-projects.com/events/seeds-saplings/.

development of an orchard community group to constitute and fundraise. Though the fruit trees have mothered their buds through another winter (to paraphrase Patrick Geddes and a slogan Jonathan and Sarah screen printed onto tote bags), there was serious friction in the process of setting up the community orchard group, which is far from resolved. We will need to wait and see what happens next. I hope the orchard might still become a place for multi-species kinship and care that extends across the communities of Huntly, human and more-than-human.

The Strathbogie Seed Collective (SSC) is one way the project lives on through a different form. The distribution of organic, open-pollinated and often heritage or heirloom seeds had been an important part of the project, as had been learning about seed saving, both vegetables and wildflowers, so we were really keen to find a way to continue to support these practices locally. The SSC emerged as a way to do this. Working with Dawn Finch, a local writer and allotmenteer, we initiated the SSC, a local seed library. Seed libraries are *commoning* projects that collect and share seeds within a community, which often preserve heirloom and distinct local varieties, by keeping those plants *in cultivation* and *out of pri-*

vatisation. Seeds can be "borrowed" from the library, used to grow a crop for the season, allowing some of the plants to go to seed. These seeds are then saved and returned to the library for others to use. A seed library's collection is usually very specific to a particular set of local circumstances, such as climate, soils, horticultural or agricultural traditions, and the interests and tastes of the people using it. Not only is it a form of activism and a commons, but also a really interesting place from which to "rethink and re-enact the relationship between economy and ecology" (Gibson-Graham and Miller, 2015, 7) through the relational practices of seed saving. Dawn has now been joined by ecological garden designer Katrina Flad, as the library's two curators. It will take a few years for the library to establish, for its membership to grow and to develop a network of seed savers who can keep the library stocked each year. So far though it has had a lot of people use it. Helping to set up the SSC led me to pursue a PhD research project on story, seeds and seed libraries, and to setting up a seed library in Helsinki, so I guess these are also ways the project has taken on different forms too.

CG: So, to wrap up, what about the carbon counting?

JA: Over three years we supported people living in Huntly to reduce their CO_2e emissions by seventy-one tonnes, which maybe feels somewhat arbitrary so for reference the average carbon footprint of a person living in the UK is eight tonnes of CO_2e. I think this is something to be acknowledged but as I discussed above I don't really see it as the main outcome of the project. It doesn't speak to, what curator Lucia Pietroiusti might call, the "analogic", those things beyond the logic of understanding the climate and ecological emergency in terms of measurable emissions. I'm happy that the project was much messier than that. I think the project began the difficult task of trying to stay with the trouble, like you mentioned earlier; it was an attempt to not avoid some of the difficult climate and ecological questions by providing smooth solutions. To deal with climate and ecological awareness and anxiety. To try and acknowledge that:

We cannot predict what might emerge from individual and collective practices of staying with the trouble, except that it holds the possibility of another world, still imperfect and impure, and another one after that. The possibility of other worlds, hospitable to hosting many worlds, might be beyond our capacity to imagine. Still, such a possibility can only arise because of our imperfect attempts to make it so (Shotwell, 2016, 204).

I do hope that the project in some small way might have nurtured some transformations along the way—it certainly did for me in ways I'm only really coming to terms with now. That we might have been able to nurture a similar sense of "practical reverence" and interdependence I felt after planting the *White Wood*, that might help us begin to work out how to get out of this mess, while staying messy, impure and imperfect.

CG: And of course, these chapbooks are also something that emerged from TiTG.

JA: Yes, a really important aspect of the project has been about exploring the garden as a place of collective investigation. A place for generating and sharing forms of communal knowledge. So, these chapbooks are a really important way for us to try and capture some of the ways of thinking and doing we explored and to share them more widely, as both documentation and as an invitation. The work has really only just begun. ...

References

Allen, Joss., and Zeiske, Claudia. *Oaks and Amity Project Report* (Huntly: Deveron Projects, 2015). Accessed online. https://www.deveron-projects.com/site_media/uploads/caroline_wendling_oaks_and_amity_report.pdf

Ang, Gey Pin., and Gatt. Caroline. "Crafting Anthropology Otherwise: Alterity and Performance". In Liana Chua and Nayaniak Mathur (eds.). *Who are "We"?: Reimagining Alterity and Affinity in Anthropology.* (New York and Oxford: Berghahn Books, 2018). 179–206.

Billimore, Yvonne., and Koitela, Jussi. *Rehearsing Hospitalities Companion 2* (Berlin and Helsinki: Archive Books and Frame Contemporary Art Finland, 2020).

Bishop, Claire. "Antagonism and Relational Aesthetics". *October* 110 (2004).

Bryant, Levi., Srnicek, Nick., and Harman, Graham (eds.). *The Speculative Turn: Continental Materialism and Realism* (Prahan: re.press, 2011).

Cooke, Lynne. "7000 Oaks". *Dia Art Foundation* (n.d.). Accessed online. http://web.mit.edu/allan-mc/www/cookebeuys.pdf

Crouch, David., and Ward, Colin. *The Allotment: Its Landscape and Culture* (Nottingham: Five Leaves Publications, 1997).

Donovan, Jared., and Gunn, Wendy. "Moving from Objects to Possibilities". In Wendy Gunn and Jared Donovan (eds.). *Design Anthropology: An Introduction* (New York and London: Routledge, 2012). 121–134.

Foster, Hal. "The Artist as Ethnographer". In Georeg Marcus and Fred Myers (eds.). *The Traffic in Culture. Refiguring Art and Anthropology* (Berkeley and London: University of California Press). 302–309.

Gatt, Caroline. "Breathing Beyond Embodiment: Exploring Emergence, Grieving and Song in Laboratory Theatre". *Body and Society* 26:2 (2020). 106–129.
—— *An Ethnography of Global Environmentalism: Becoming Friends of the Earth* (New York and Lon-

don: Routledge, 2018).

——"The anthropologist as member of the ensemble: Anthropological experiments with theatre makers". In Alex Flynn and Jonas Tinius (eds.). *Anthropology, Theatre, and Development: The Transformative Potential of Performance* (New York and London: Palgrave, 2015). 334–356.

Gell, Alfred. "Vogel's Net: Traps as Artworks and Artworks as Traps". *Journal of Material Culture* 1:1 (1996). 15–38.

Gibson, J.K., Rose, D.B., and Fincher, R (eds.). *Manifesto for Living in the Anthropocene* (Punctum Books: New York, 2015).

Gruppuso, Paolo. "Edenic Views in Wetland Conservation: Nature and Agriculture in the Fogliano Area, Italy". *Conservation & Society* 16:4 (2018). 397–408.

Haraway, Donna. *Staying with the Trouble: Making Kin in the Chthulucene* (Durham: Duke University Press, 2016).

Ingold, Tim., and Hallam, Elizabeth. "Creativity

and Cultural Improvisation: An Introduction". In Tim Ingold and Elizabeth Hallam (eds.). *Creativity and Cultural Improvisation* (New York and Oxford: Berg, 2007).

Kester, Grant. *The One and the Many: Contemporary Collaborative Art in a Global Context* (Durham and London; Duke University Press, 2011).

Le Guin, Ursula K. "Carrier Bag Theory of Fiction". *Dancing at the Edge of the World* (Grove Press: New York, 1989).
——*The Lathe of Heaven* (London : Gollanz, 2018)
——National Book Foundation's Medal for Distinguished Contribution to American Letters at the 65th National Book Awards (November 19, 2014) [video]. https://youtu.be/Et9Nf-rsALk

Macpherson, Alan. "Of Time and Trees'. In Caroline Wendling (ed.). *White Wood* (Huntly: Deveron Projects, 2016). Accessed online. https://www.deveron-projects.com/site_media/uploads/Alan%20 McPherson%20Of%20Time%20and%20Trees. pdf

Meulemans, Germain. "The lure of pedogenesis: an anthropological foray into making urban soils in contemporary France". PhD Thesis, University of Aberdeen, Aberdeen (2017).

Mikulak, Michael. *The Politics of the Pantry: Stories, Food, and Social Change* (Montreal and Kingston: McGill-Queen's University Press, 2013).

Monbiot, George. *Out of the Wreckage: A Politics for an Age of Crisis* (Verso: UK; ebook edn, 2017).

Myers, Natasha. "From the Anthropocene to the Planthroposcene: Designing Gardens for Plant/People Involution". *History and Anthropology* 28:3 (2017). Accessed online. https://www.academia.edu/32277553/From_the_Anthropocene_to_the_Planthroposcene_Designing_Gardens_for_Plant_People_Involution_Response_to_Battaglia

Safier, Neil. "Global Knowledge on the Move: Itineraries, Amerindian Narratives, and Deep Histories of Science". *Isis* 101:1 (2010). 133–145.

Sansi, Roger. *Art, Anthropology and the Gift* (London: Bloomsbury, 2015).

Silverman, Sydel. *Three Bells of Civilization: The Life of an Italian Hill Town* (New York: Columbia University Press, 1975).

Theodossopoulos, Dimitrios. *Troubles with Turtles: Cultural Understandings of the Environment on a Greek Island* (New York and Oxford: Berghahn Books, 2003).

Tsing, Anna., Swanson, Heather., Gan, Elaine., and Bubandt, Nils (eds.). *The Arts of Living on a Damaged Planet* (Minneapolis and London: University of Minnesota Press, 2017).

Willes, Margaret. *The Gardens of the British Working Class* (New Haven: Yale University Press, 2014).

Joss Allen can be found at the edges of the garden, amongst the weeds and compost heaps. He is an artworker and gardener exploring how creative practices can shape earthy politics, community economies and ecological ways of being in playful, radical, responsive and meaningful ways. He is interested in collaborations across disciplines, peer education, storytelling and community building. His work has been influenced by his time as a support worker for adults with autism, a labourer on an organic farm and a refuse collector, among others. Joss currently lives in Helsinki, Finland where he is in the process of establishing a local seed library and pursuing a PhD research project on seed saving and story.

Caroline Gatt is Senior Research Fellow, Institute of Cultural Anthropology and European Ethnology, University of Graz and Co-Investigator on the project '(Musical) Improvisation and Ethics' funded by the Austrian Science Fund. She is an anthropologist and performer, and her research interests include collaborative anthropology, environmentalism, laboratory theatre, design anthropology, ontological politics and ethical self-formation. She is author of 'Breathing Beyond Embodiment: Exploring Emergence, Grief and Song in Laboratory Theatre' (2020), and An Ethnography of Global Environmentalism: Becoming Friends of the Earth *(2018) and editor of the special issue of Collaborative Anthropologies 'Considering Onto/Epistemology in Collaboration' (2018), and* The Voices of the Pages *(2017)* .

Town is the Garden

A community food growing project, *of sorts*.

For three years the Town is the Garden team could be found at the margins of the garden. Amongst the weeds and compost heaps, they explored what it might mean to *think with* the garden. Through crafting gardens, vegetable plots and orchards they attempted to rethink how a community might feed itself as it faces up to the global climate and ecological emergency. Through the processes of learning and sharing skills in relation to growing food, from planting seeds to preserving the harvest, they asked how we might also begin to pay better attention to the entanglement of human and more-than-human worlds. They asked how might the garden be a site of both resistance and resilience? A place for *thinking* and *doing* ecology, otherwise.

This is *Story I* in a collection of seven chapbooks by the *Town is the Garden* that attempt to capture some of the diverse ways of thinking, doing and knowing the project explored with some of the people they explored them with. It includes contributions from Eleanor Brown and Alexandra Falter (*Plants*), Jonathan Baxter & Sarah Gittins (*Orchard*), Joe Crowdy (*Garden*), Dawn Finch

(*Seeds*), Maria Puig de la Bellacasa (*Compost*), and Joss Allen, Caroline Gatt and Elisabetta Rattalino (*Story*). With cover illustrations by Jamie Johnson.

The Town is the Garden team included: Joss Allen (2017–20), Rhian Davies (2019–20), Caroline Gatt (2018–20), Camille Sineau (2017–18), and Lindy Young (2017–19).

https://www.deveron-projects.com/town-garden

The *Town is the Garden* team would like to thank everyone who contributed to these chapbooks and Footprint Workers Cooperative for their exceptional printing skills.

A massive thank you to everyone at Deveron Projects, staff, board and interns (too many to name), especially Petra Pennington, Robyn Wolsey and Claudia Zeiske—for their support and guidance—and the Neep & Okra Kitchen team—with whom we latterly shared space and ideas with. To Alex Severn, our wonderful intern, on a student placement from the University of Aberdeen. To our generous funders Aberdeenshire Council, Action Earth, Climate Challenge Fund, Community Growing Fund, Creative Scotland, Finnis Scott Foundation, Groundwork, and Grow Wild. Many thanks to the Aberdeenshire Environmental

Forum for awarding the Green Butterfly Award to Huntly Town, partly in recognition of the work of the *Town is the Garden* project. The award gave the team great encouragement.

We would like to thank everyone who took part in the *Town is the Garden* project, for their generosity, patience and support. In particular those who contributed to the programme: Matt Aitkenhead, Andy Smith, Charlie Ashton, Grace Banks, Rosa Bevan and James Reid, John Bolland, Stephen Brandes, Alan Carter, Karen Collins, Doug Cookson, Uist Corrigan, Bob Donald, David Easton and Jane Lockyer, Petra/Patrick Geddes, Katrina Flad, Marguerite Fleming, Vicky Flood, David Foubister, Cristina Grasseni, Charlie Hanks, Margaret and Andrew Lear, Leslie Mabon, John Malster, Ann Miller, Miranda Montgomery, Bryan Morrison, Joshua Msika, Lorna Patterson, Chris Pepper, Annabel Pinker, Ian Scott, Pat Scott, Christine Steiner, Emma Stewart, Katie Stewart, Andrew Tassell, Leanne Townsend, Nikki and James Yoxall, David Watts, the Grow it, Cook it, Eat it team at BBC Radio Scotland, and everyone at the Scottish Sculpture Workshop.

And finally to Yvonne Billimore, Richard Muscat and Mariuccia Muscat, for all kinds of care, encouragement, sharp-eyes and support throughout.

Town is the Garden: Story I
Published by Deveron Projects and Intellect in 2021

Edited by Joss Allen and Caroline Gatt
Layout by Joss Allen
Cover illustrations by Jamie Johnson
Printed and bound by Footprint Workers Cooperative, Leeds

Typeface: Adobe Casion Pro / Garamond Pro
Paper: Context Natural / Evercopy Plus

ISBN 978-1-907115-37-0

Deveron Projects is a company limited by guarantee, registered in Scotland No. SC391020 and a registered Scottish Charity No. SC024261

83

Town is the Garden Chapbooks
Deveron Projects and Intellect

Plants
/
Eleanor Brown and Alexandra Falter

Plants

Foraging, an incidental mindfulness practice
Eleanor Brown

*Relationships in motion with plants and
people in the Bolivian Andes*
Alexandra Falter

Foraging, an incidental mindfulness practice
Eleanor Brown

Resilience emerges from biodiversity, if we value this in our bodies then we will value it in our environment.

~ Eleanor Brown, this volume

Every now and then I realise I am engaged in ritual. The revelation sneaks up on me surfacing from seasonal habits. I am immersed in a practice heavy with meaningful attention, devoted. The haptic cognition or touchable experience connects me to past rituals, deepening my relationship to the plants. It is joyful and restorative.

The pandemic and ensuing lockdown has given me the headspace to fully embrace these foraging meditations, reclaiming them on a personal level and bringing to mind a much younger me encountering these plants for the first time.[1] For several years now I have expanded this practice to include others through workshops and walks. Although I love the knowledge sharing and the vicarious thrill when someone makes a new wild connection, it has at times resulted in hurried harvesting distracted by thoughts of what recipes and musings to prepare and share. I am so grateful to the wild places for getting me through these strange times and I would like to invite you to consider deepening your

---

1. This text was written during the first wave of the coronavirus pandemic in the UK in 2020 .

connection to the green world where you may also find peace of mind and nourishment for your body.

Plants are our allies. It is more important than ever to support robust immune systems, communities and ecosystems, and there is no better way to do this than by increasing the variety of wild food and medicines in our diet. Resilience emerges from biodiversity, if we value this in our bodies then we will value it in our environment.

I hope to give you a glimpse into my foraging year featuring plants always present in my larder or apothecary, our co-evolutionary partners that by their proximity invite us to make use of their abundant nutrition and medicine...

Spring

Plucking cleavers for my brew I become aware how the tender leaf has developed bristles that tug gently at my skin.

Emerging shoots and succulent first leaves offer spring tonics to wake us from our winter torpor. From March, onwards I gather cleavers most days to use fresh in a cold infusion, adding a few sprigs of peppermint gone feral by the stream at the edge of my garden. On its own, the flavour is reminiscent of cucumber with an embodied nutritional punch.

Cleavers (Galium aparine) cold infusion

Gather your cleavers tops, nipping each plant at the point where the whorls of leaves start to brown or have been nibbled—I often count each one usually getting to fifty. Chop the fresh plants and add to a litre jar with a little water for lubrication. I use a wooden cocktail muddler to bruise and release the goodness. Then fill to the top with water, stir well and close the lid. Keep in the fridge for at least a few hours (overnight is best) and strain into a glass to drink throughout the day.

The first shoots of sweet cicely (Myrrhis odorata) are tender and sweet with a mild taste of aniseed, delicious juiced with apples or roasted whole with rhubarb. Keep a close eye on sweet cicely, flowers and seeds set early and you want to try the seeds while fresh and green as a wayside nibble or a perfect substitute for fennel in masala chai and curries.

Favourite springtime greens are chickweed, dandelion leaves, ground elder, common hogweed, sorrel, curled dock, plantain and wild garlic. You may notice them when you start to clear your garden for planting. Use fresh in stir fries and salsa verde or stock up on wild pesto. My biggest jars and freezer space are reserved though for the nutritional powerhouse that is nettle (Urtica dioica). Nettle harvest begins in spring and continues till summers end, pre-flowering leaves cut and come again. Blanched and pulped for the freezer to be added to soups, stews, breads, pastas and even cakes. Dried for strong infusions and to add to allergy tea mixes with elderflower, plantain and yarrow.

Summer

Gathering rosebay willowherb leaves for my Ivan tea, the smell of meadowsweet draws my mind to my next task at hand.

Midsummer, a time of flowering. This publication documents the wonderful project Town is the Garden, the town in focus being Huntly. For this reason, I must mention linden (Tilia sp.). The tree that nurtures community, planted as avenues and bordering village greens following a long-held tradition. The aromatics of the linden flowers are potent nervous system relaxants. Town centres were the venues for community meetings and consensual decisions are easier to reach when all are calm and focussed. I love the fresh flower tea and I also dry the flowers, including the papery bracts, for winter evenings. It is the perfect brew to release the tensions of the day. Other aromatics to consider are dog rose, Japanese rose, meadowsweet, elderflower, sweet cicely, flowering currant, rowan and hawthorn blossom, pineapple weed, wild pansy and yarrow. Dry them for teas; your future self will be grateful to have a shelf full of colour and aromas to pick and mix from throughout the dark months. Infuse in honey, try wild floral champagnes that employ the natural yeasts present on the flowers. Fresh picked and muddled in a cocktail or even just fizzy water is a refreshing and instant treat. For good shelf life and medicinal administration tinctures and elixirs are a great craft to learn.

Dog rose elixir (Rosa canina)

My favourite floral elixir. The aromatic oils are elusive and there are astringent tannins to avoid so the process requires care, I find it engaging and well worth the effort. It is a precious substance sparingly administered when someone needs uplifting. I planted a dog rose bush in my garden many years ago and when in bloom I harvest the flowers every day, if you hold all the petals and pull gently they release leaving behind the reproductive parts that will produce the rosehip in autumn. I submerge them immediately in vodka where they infuse overnight then strain and discard the spent petals just before adding the new day's harvest. This continues for about two weeks until the flowering passes. To finish I lightly warm honey and stir in to the tincture, twenty-five percent honey to seventy-five percent tincture, before bottling in dark glass.

Summers end, late August in the pinewoods and the heather is in full bloom, a flower that can be harvested in abundance, cured (essentially just bruised and dried) and added to your favourite black tea. Robert Burns enjoyed this with blaeberry leaves and wild thyme. If you are a tea jenny it is worth exploring the practice of curing and fermenting wild native leaves and flowers as an alternative to traditional Chinese teas, rosebay willowherb (Chamaenerion angustafolium) and raspberry leaf are good choices to begin with. Research Ivan tea and learn from the Russians how the curing and fermenting of rosebay willowherb leaves can develop deeply fruity flavours in a tea that works well served with a splash of milk. [2]

Among the heather is where the early berries are found, blaes and cowberries. The blaes I mostly eat fresh from the bush while the cowberries make a tasty, vibrant red jam. Some plants flower throughout summer so there's still time to harvest aromatics, notably pineapple weed (Matricaria discoidia - our wild chamomile) and yarrow (Achillea millefolium). More seeds are on the menu now. I dry plantain (Plantago sp.) and curled dock (Rumex crispus) seeds to grind and add to breads and crackers for extra flavour, B vitamins and omega oils. I make a jar or two of nettle seed gomasio every year and harvest common hogweed seed to roast and grind for cake, biscuits and chai. Nettle seeds are prescribed by herbalists for adrenal

2. See *Orchard* in this collection for a rosebay willowherb tea recipe.

exhaustion so this condiment provides an energy boost while reducing salt intake.

Nettle Seed Gomasio
4 tablespoons sesame seeds
2 tablespoon nettle seeds
1 tablespoon sea salt

Japanese Gomasio usually contains seaweed so feel free to add if that's something you have to hand.

Toast the sesame seeds on a low heat in the oven or in a dry cast iron frying pan, stir often to prevent from burning. Grind sesame and nettle seeds together with the salt.

Autumn

Walking the woodland path leads to remembering and I find myself in the stand of birch where the golden chanterelles are ready for harvest.

September and the brambles and tree berries are full with juice. I spend the entire month tickling berries from their stalks. Thinking of it now evokes the smell of wood smoke with evenings cool enough to light the stove, the autumn sunsets filling the space with an orange glow and baskets brimming with bunches of hawthorn, elder, rowan, rosehips and sloes. The rhythm of the work is meditative and soothing. I'll spend many hours listening to music or podcasts while I work, the anthocyanins staining my fingertips, a colourful expression of the potent antiviral tonics our bodies look for in the winter. Feral quince, apples and plums can often be found to supplement the various jams, chutneys, sauces, fruit leathers, spicy cordials and infused vinegars that these berries are destined to become. A recipe below but a reminder too that they can simply be dried or frozen for storage to make use of later in the year. It's a busy time for the forager as the mushroom hunt is fully underway and I enjoy adding freshly sautéed chanterelles, ceps and hedgehog mushrooms to autumn dinners.

Elderberry balsamic vinegar
400g ripe elderberries
(Sambucus nigra)
500ml red wine vinegar
700g cane sugar
Put destalked berries in a bowl and pound lightly with a potato masher. Pour over

the red wine vinegar, cover with muslin or a lid and leave for 5 days. Shake or stir each day. Strain through a fine sieve and pour the liquid into a saucepan. Add the sugar and warm until dissolved. Keep stirring so the sugar doesn't burn or start to caramelise. Bring to a rolling boil and simmer for 10 minutes. Pour into sterilised bottles and cap using cork or plastic lined caps otherwise they will corrode due to the vinegar.

Winter

Mid-winter and the colourful turkey tails are bringing dead wood to life.

Deep winter when the plants appear to be asleep but as long as the earth is soft we can harvest the deep tap roots that are pungent with bitter medicine and rich with minerals. It is illegal to uproot a wild plant without the landowner's permission but these plants are often considered weeds and are likely well established at the edge of your garden— welcome them in. Curled dock, dandelion and burdock (Arctium lappa) are a triplet that I like to infuse in apple cider vinegar. This is the perfect medium for dissolving minerals increasing their bioavailability. Use in salad dressings and simmer the infused roots in stews. It's a good time too for spotting fungi like turkey tail and chaga.

The following recipe is for the decadent Dandy Chai. The spice mix works just as well with chaga or turkey tail mushroom tea or in the deeply delicious spiced elderberry rob—all wonderful winter tonics. When you get to know your native spices from the carrot family you can substitute them in the mix.

Dandy Chai

    8 tablespoons dandelion root
    (Taraxacum officinale)
    20 cardamom pods
    1 tbsp. whole pink peppercorns
    1 tbsp. whole black peppercorns
    2 tbsp. fennel seeds
    1 tbsp. coriander seeds
    1 tsp whole cloves
    3 cinnamon sticks
    4 tbsp. chopped crystallised ginger

Roast the spices except the crystallised ginger, in a preheated oven at 160 degrees

Celsius or on the stovetop in a cast iron frying pan, check and move them often, when fragrant grind but not to a powder and combine with the dandelion root and candied ginger. Simmer one tablespoon measure per mug of water for 15 mins or more. Strain and add milk and honey to taste.

Being held in these complex relationships is fundamental to my emotional wellbeing. With the shifting energetics of the seasons they connect me to a time and place, a standpoint from which I can make sense of my world.

Resources

I cannot overstate the need to be 100 per cent accurate with your identification of a plant or fungi before choosing to eat it. Cross referencing your sources and reconfirming your identification many times is important. Learn the features that distinguish a plant from their poisonous lookalikes. The carrot family, mentioned often in this article, should be carefully studied throughout the growing season, the poisonous members are deadly and bear much resemblance to the edibles. Learn too the parts that are safe to use and if processing is required to neutralize toxins or improve flavour. Common names can be informative but deceptive as they change from region to region. There are a great many excellent books, websites and social media groups available. My favourites are listed below but again do not rely on one source.

Wild food books:

Irving, Miles. *The Forager* (UK: Ebury Press, 2009)

Mabey, Richard. *Food for Free* (UK: Collins, 2012).

Any of the Roger Philips guides.

Wright, John. *The Edible Seashore: River Cottage Handbook 5* (London: Bloomsbury, 2009).
——*Hedgerow: River Cottage Hanbook 7* (Bloomsbury: UK, 2010).
——*Mushrooms: River Cottage Handbook 1* (London: Bloomsbury, 2007).
——*The Forager's Calendar* (UK: Profile Books, 2019).

Books on plant remedies:

Grieves, Maude. *A Modern Herbal.* Written over 100 years ago, this book is still a useful guide to plant uses and is a joy to browse for folklore and historical info.

Mase, Guido. *The Wild Medicine Solution: Healing with Aromatic, Bitter and Tonic Plants* (USA: Healing Arts Press, 2013).

Hoffman, David. *The Holistic Herbal* (UK: Thorsons, 1990).

Useful websites:

Some people kindly curate a website of the work of Maude Grieves: https://botanical.com

Great detailed information on making tinctures, syrups and teas: https://theherbarium. wordpress.com/

The following site is a phenomenal resource, a database of plant information, identification and uses: https://pfaf.org

15

16

Relationships in motion with plants and people in the Bolivian Andes
Alexandra Falter

[H]uman-plant relationships rather than being smooth, complementary, or somehow intuitive due to some sort of co-inhabitation, are actually quite often disruptive and problematic.

~ Alexandra Falter

This text explores human-plant relationships, in particular between plants and people in contemporary Bolivia. The terminology human-plant *relationships* or *relations* may sound pretentious and somewhat alienated from the lived experience of people. But this is not so. What these terms describe is first of all some sort of connection between people and plants. The terms are part of a wider area of research which is not trying to romanticise human-plant entanglements. Note how although it is fair to say that human life depends on plant life, we may well observe current worldwide human activities that threaten plant life dramatically. We may deduce from this that human-plant relationships rather than being smooth, complementary, or somehow intuitive due to some sort of co-inhabitation, are actually quite often disruptive and problematic. So instead the research in this field poses a variety of questions that may foster insights about human-plant relationships. For instance: How do people come to use plants in different places? How do plants take over spaces (for example, urban ones)? How can social scientists provide anthropologically rich examinations of phytochemical and shamanic experiences of tropical forest people? How do scientists working for the Millennium Seed Bank perceive plant life and conceptualise "wild places,"? And specific to my own research, asking: How are human-plant interactions integrated or embedded into Andean structures of existence with other (living) beings?

In Bolivia I searched for insights and possible answers to these questions. One question in particular captivated my interest: *How do people grow into medicinal plant knowledge?* By closely examining local circumstances I came to work with local and traditional health experts (in Spanish *médicos tradicionales*), laypeople, and scientists in the La Paz department. Bolivia is a country with diverse ecosystems, ranging from the high plateaus (*altiplano*), the humid and dry valleys (*Yungas* and *valles secos*), to the lowlands of the east (*tierras bajas*), rich cultural settings, and many linguistic groups. It is home to a variety of medical and pharmaceutical practices. Among Andean experts with medical expertise are the internationally recognised *Kallawayas* who apply vegetal, animal, and mineral-based recipes as well as ceremonial practices not only in the treatment of individual patients, but also in the restoring and strengthen-

20

ing of communities whose relationship with the spiritual world had been disrupted. However, there are several other knowledgeable groups and individuals who are well versed in either growing, collecting, experimenting or otherwise engaging with medicinal plants, and/or engaging in ceremonial practices. These are, to give just a few examples, Aymara-speaking Amautas and Yatiris, female and male midwives, herbalists, mestizo curanderos, naturopaths, Quechua-speaking Qulliris. Interestingly, the manipulation of plants with curative properties and the use of plant-based remedies are not confined to rural areas. Urban spaces are equally fascinating to look at and as important as rural spaces for understanding Bolivia's medical landscape.

As in many other Latin American countries, in Bolivia many people decide to move from their rural place of origin to a large city in the search of better labour, and hence economic opportunities. However, there are some nuances and differences compared with neighbouring countries. For instance, highland Bolivians regularly dwell between their urban households and rural homes of origin, either to visit relatives, to fulfil their community obligations, or to participate in religious festivities.

21

Equally, many local and traditional health practitioners have moved to urban centres where they offer their therapeutic and ceremonial services, not only to fellows, but also to townspeople who look for beneficial alternatives. People choose them for various reasons. One reason is the inadequate and expensive biomedical health system which consists in public and private health services. Both are not readily accessible for everyone. A considerable part of the population hasn't got the necessary financial means to meet the costs for medical consultancies, surgeries, laboratory tests, pharmaceuticals, and other medical appliances such as medical oxygen gas cylinders.

How does this relate to human-plant relationships? As mentioned previously, neither the medical practices of traditional health practitioners nor the acquisition of medicinal plants are confined to rural areas or the domestic space but can be found in the cities where they are inscribed in the public sphere: in markets, street stalls and individual spaces for medical consultation in different neighborhoods. The medicinal plants that are sold in the cities come from various regions of Bolivia, but mostly from its humid valleys. Researchers have found over a hundred purchasable plants at urban markets and including various plant families such as Anacardiaceae, Asteraceae, Betulaceae, Caprifoliaceae, Caryophyllaceae, Ephedraceae, Euphorbiaceae, just to mention a few. However, much of these plant resources are being collected close to roads. Moreover, they are being collected mostly by less experienced collectors. For this reason, the traditional and local health practitioners I interviewed preferred to grow their plants when possible in their own gardens, in shared plant nurseries or they have tried themselves to get the needed quantities from their rural places of origin and other personal collection sites. This habit of getting medicinal plants from "non-contaminated places", as they would put it when we talked, is inseparable from their medical and pharmaceutical practice, and also inseparable from a particular concept of being in the world. In other words, on the one hand the plant-based remedy and the result of its application can only be as good as the quality of its ingredients. On the other hand, a plant within Andean cosmology is not just a plant but a living being provided by mother earth and father sun, that is there to be taken but also to be nurtured and thanked for. These Andean medical practitioners or healers have been "growing into" medicinal plant knowledge over many years or even, in some cases, from as early as infancy. They "grow into" medical knowledge by living in relation with plants, always guided by other experienced health practitioners, and very much influenced by shared communal traditions and beliefs such as faith in ancestors, father sun, God, mother earth, mountain spirits, Saints, and Virgin Mary. Instead of saying Andean medical practitioners "acquire" medical knowledge, I use "growing into" because it describes best that this knowledge has been nurtured over a long period of time under careful supervision by members of the terrestrial and spiritual world. This carefully nurtured knowledge stays in line with all beings that in Andean cosmology are worth of respect and nurture.

Taking this very actual religious and spiritual context into consideration means that living organisms in general, and medicinal plants in particular, are far more than raw material for human use. They are gifts which depend upon care and nurturing. For these medicinal plants to work and to persist into the future requires that people maintain a good relationship with mother earth, also known as Pachamama, and also other religious entities, through ritual offerings. These offerings symbolize

24

a reciprocal feeding, for example in form of a *mesa*, a feast. In the Andean context anthropologists have long emphasized the relation between *bringing up children* and growing plants and describe all these as *relationships of nurturing*. This is very much the position of the anthropologist Tim Ingold when he writes and suggests that we (Ingold refers to the farmer) don't make crops, but "set up conditions of development within which plants and animals take on their particular forms" (Ingold 2011, 77). The most famous example from the Andes is the growing of potatoes. The potato plant is spread throughout the Andes, but its growth and its variety depends highly on human intervention. At the same time people in the Andes depend largely on potatoes for subsistence as well as a means for exchange between kin. It is this relationship which I call *mutual nurturing*. *Mutual* because plants and people enhance each other's growth and well-being, and *nurturing* because people take care and prepare the conditions for plants to grow.

Having said this, I restate that this is not a romanticising perspective but one that considers that plants and people do not exist separated or isolated from each other but entangled in a shared environment. I am not referring here to the envi-

25

ronment in terms of global discourses but much more in the sense of the environment of our lived experiences. The consequence is that we may experience considerably different "environments." From an experiential point of view or phenomenological perspective it is very different if I live in southern Germany, the valleys of Bolivia or northern Scotland. Furthermore, depending if we live in the countryside or an urban place, we may share this environment with plants (and of course animals and other organisms) to varying degrees and in very different ways. However, we humans are never detached from nature, we are part of it, even if we may act as if we weren't, which then often results in treating plants and animals as objects or resources rather than as beings or organisms with whom we share this world. I won't claim that this objectification of nature doesn't happen in Bolivia. Before the emergence of Covid-19, Bolivia was considered one of the fastest growing economies in Latin America, a relatively stable economy while still being a "poor" country according to economists' global comparisons. Until recently people were purchasing commodities of all kinds, mostly imported from China, Brazil and Argentina. In other words, Bolivia is in many ways a very traditional

26

place, but also a place that is thoroughly connected through international networks and markets. As a result, Andean and other indigenous concepts of life are no longer solely in charge but must coexist alongside other—quite often objectifying—world views, and powerful economic interests. Hence, the experience of environments in Bolivia is also highly diverse including traditional Andean and biomedical understandings of plants.

Currently, the country is facing political uncertainty. The virus keeps the country on its toes at a time when new elections are due, and members of the previous ruling party are trying to regain power after their president was forced by the people to resign. The former president Evo Morales once gave a speech filled with great expectations as he defended the rights of the Pachamama. However, Bolivia is far from being a country where the rights of mother earth are being respected. While politicians are celebrating indigeneity and vowing to preserve and protect Pachamama. At the same time corruption, large-scale exploitation of natural resources and the destruction of diverse habitats are the order of the day.

The point I want to make here is that respectful relationships, and in my research I refer specifically

27

to human-plant relationships, exist as long there are places where they can come into being and be shared. The relationships with plants of the people I worked with are deeply rooted in their gardening practices, the growing of crops on fields, the maintenance of their plots, herding their animals and in the case of medicinal plants also in their long walks along the various paths in the mountains, the valleys, plateaus, and lowlands. Various medicinal plants grow in human and animal disturbed places, that means not only in gardens and plots, but also close to roads, pathways, and even waste sites. And of course, there are other places more distant from densely populated human areas; places one has to look for on deep slopes, close to rocks, forests or some other hidden places. For the *médicos tradicionales* who have moved to cities this long-term experience is vital but difficult if not to say impossible to share with the next generation to the same extent. Taking the cities of El Alto and La Paz (which are the destination for many people from the countryside) as example, there a barely any public green spaces or gardens in which this relationship can be nurtured or shared with children and grandchildren; hardly any places where they can sow, collect or name plants and so forth with the next generation.

In Aucapata municipality, a dry valley of the Andes, in which I spent various months during 2016, I myself entered into a closer relationship with plants by growing into medicinal plant knowledge. I did so by getting into a different, more direct, practical, and sensual relationship with plants compared to the rather observational methods I was used to previously. When it comes to plants, *knowing* is not possible without involving all senses. It was with don Silvino the local healer (known as *curandero*) and bone expert (*huesero*) that I got to know various medicinal plants growing in the region. We used to walk for hours throughout the seasons—continuously touching, smelling and tasting *cuchu cuchu, chojo chojo, ch'ullku, ch'illkha, amorseco, atencora, achicoria* and many other plants—in order for me to get to know, to recognize, to distinguish them, and to slowly memorize their names. Getting to know medicinal plants not only within the space of a garden but beyond is only one of the many aspects that makes up the relationship between plants and people, and in particular the relationship of people and medicinal plants. Further aspects are the collection, the drying and the processing of the plants, for example, in form of herbal teas, poultices, and ointments. Finally knowing how to ingest plants with curative properties as well as applying them on others is also how the relationship with plants is grown. All of these require time, and as mentioned previously they require the adequate places and settings where these relations can unfold.

Lastly, it is experience that accompanies all of what has been mentioned so far. Medicinal plants are first and foremost plants, which become medicinal as a result of relating to them. Experience is what strengthens this relationship. Traditional and local health experts have much to say about this. Don Silvino repeatedly told me that plants are both effective and harmful; it all depends on the parts of the plant one uses, the quantity, the preparation, the combination with other plants, the person's specific bodily characteristics, improper application of internal or external use, and an individual's beliefs. He once described one example of how harmful plants can be as we were walking close to an edge of ch'illkha shrubs (*Baccharis latifolia* (Ruiz & Pav.), Asteraceae). He told me about a woman who had lost her life after she ingested a particular plant, she used it internally. She constantly felt anger towards her husband and

30

children about everyday life quarrels. This provoked irregular menstruation, which she hoped to get under control by drinking ch'illkha mate. How much she drank of it is uncertain, but she passed away because of it (don Silvino, pers. comm., February 2016). However, used externally ch'illkha is known to be very effective. Don Silvino does not use ch'illkha on its own, but mixed with other ingredients to improve its effectiveness, especially when treating fractures. He treats fractures by carefully palpating the injured body part. Through skilful and gentle touching, he gets a feeling of the damage and the position of bones, which sometimes have to repositioned.

To conclude, such interest in human-plant relationships derives from a particular, long-standing academic concern about the intensified environmental challenges that humanity is facing. As anthropologists Anna Tsing and Nils Bubandt suggest, "We have entered a new geologic epoch, defined by human disturbance of the earth's ecosystems—the Anthropocene" (Tsing 2015, 7). Twenty years ago, in 2000, the term was widely popularised by atmospheric chemists Paul J. Crutzen and Eugene Stoermer. In this regard, Anna Tsing demonstrates that both social scientists and conservation biologists are interested in finding out what it means to live in a "multispecies world" (Tsing 2005, 172) and other anthropologists like Eduardo Kohn ask, "What kind of anthropology can emerge through this form of defamiliarising the human?" (Kohn 2013, 125). To contribute to this field of inquiry with examples from Bolivia—a country that, on the one hand, is facing severe environmental issues due to monocultures and massive resource extractions, and, on the other hand, claims to protect "mother earth"– is fascinating. The paradigms are shifting in anthropology and the ethnographic subject is being reconsidered. Anthropological research is partially moving away from the "anthropos", the human, towards the more-than-human or other-than-human. Whereas for one century the main focus of interest lay on cultural materiality and complexity of human past and current societies around the world, anthropologists started thinking and writing about humans in different ways, for example as organisms among other organisms inhabiting this planet. In this sense, humans are anthropologically understood as a part of the environment, not separated from it, and henceforth, not above but among other living organisms. And as such it is finally academically accepted that humans stay in relation to other living beings. In practice, this has always been the case.

References

Bussmann, Rainer W., Narel Y. Paniagua-Zambrana, Laura Araceli Moya Huanca, and Robbie Hart. "Changing Markets – Medicinal Plants in the Markets of La Paz and El Alto, Bolivia". *Journal of Ethnopharmacology* 193 (2016), 76-95.

Crutzen, Paul., and Stoermer, Eugene. "The 'Anthropocene'". *Global Change Newsletter* 41 (2000), 17–18.

Ingold, Tim. *The Perception of the Environment: Essays on Livelihood, Dwelling and Skill,* 2nd ed. (London: Routledge, 2011).

Kohn, Eduardo. *How Forests Think: Toward an Anthropology Beyond the Human* (Berkeley and London: University of California Press, 2013).

Tsing, Anna. *Friction: An Ethnography of Global Connection* (Princeton: Princeton University Press, 2005).
———"Catachresis for the Anthropocene: Three Papers on Productive Misplacements". *AURA working papers* 1, no. AURA's opening. More-

than-Human (2015), 2-10.

36

Eleanor Brown is a forager and fermenter based in Aberdeenshire, northeast Scotland. She is an occasional poster @fermentedforager on Facebook and Instagram and you can contact her at fermentedforager@gmail.com. Eleanor is a member of the Forager's Association and recommends browsing the members' directory for access to a huge body of knowledge in the form of events and links to their individual sites. https://www.foragers-association.org.uk

Alexandra Falter is an anthropologist currently working for a German child protection organisation where she supports children and adolescents in their schooling. Education in all its rich facets is her passion and collaboration her preferred tool to advocate for it. She has previously concluded her PhD degree at the University of Aberdeen. Her project took her to Bolivia where she carried out long-term research enabling her to explore the manifold connections between education, health, and environment in the Andes. Having family in Bolivia keeps her moving back and forth between Europe and Latin America. Preferably physically, but also very much theoretically, and today simply digitally.

Town is the Garden

A community food growing project, *of sorts*.

For three years the Town is the Garden team could be found at the margins of the garden. Amongst the weeds and compost heaps, they explored what it might mean to *think with* the garden. Through crafting gardens, vegetable plots and orchards they attempted to rethink how a community might feed itself as it faces up to the global climate and ecological emergency. Through the processes of learning and sharing skills in relation to growing food, from planting seeds to preserving the harvest, they asked how we might also begin to pay better attention to the entanglement of human and more-than-human worlds. They asked how might the garden be a site of both resistance and resilience? A place for *thinking* and *doing* ecology, otherwise.

This is *Plants* in a collection of seven chapbooks by the *Town is the Garden* that attempt to capture some of the diverse ways of thinking, doing and knowing the project explored with some of the people they explored them with. It includes contributions from Eleanor Brown and Alexandra Falter (*Plants*), Jonathan Baxter & Sarah Gittins (*Orchard*), Joe Crowdy (*Garden*), Dawn Finch

(*Seeds*), Maria Puig de la Bellacasa (*Compost*), and Joss Allen, Caroline Gatt and Elisabetta Rattalino (*Story*). With cover illustrations by Jamie Johnson.

The Town is the Garden team included: Joss Allen (2017–20), Rhian Davies (2019–20), Caroline Gatt (2018–20), Camille Sineau (2017–18), and Lindy Young (2017–19).

https://www.deveron-projects.com/town-garden

The *Town is the Garden* team would like to thank everyone who contributed to these chapbooks and Footprint Workers Cooperative for their exceptional printing skills.

A massive thank you to everyone at Deveron Projects, staff, board and interns (too many to name), especially Petra Pennington, Robyn Wolsey and Claudia Zeiske—for their support and guidance—and the Neep & Okra Kitchen team—with whom we latterly shared space and ideas with. To Alex Severn, our wonderful intern, on a student placement from the University of Aberdeen. To our generous funders Aberdeenshire Council, Action Earth, Climate Challenge Fund, Community Growing Fund, Creative Scotland, Finnis Scott Foundation, Groundwork, and Grow Wild. Many thanks to the Aberdeenshire Environmental Fo-

40

rum for awarding the Green Butterfly Award to Huntly Town, partly in recognition of the work of the *Town is the Garden* project. The award gave the team great encouragement.

We would like to thank everyone who took part in the *Town is the Garden* project, for their generosity, patience and support. In particular those who contributed to the programme: Matt Aitkenhead, Andy Smith, Charlie Ashton, Grace Banks, Rosa Bevan and James Reid, John Bolland, Stephen Brandes, Alan Carter, Karen Collins, Doug Cookson, Uist Corrigan, Bob Donald, David Easton and Jane Lockyer, Petra/Patrick Geddes, Katrina Flad, Marguerite Fleming, Vicky Flood, David Foubister, Cristina Grasseni, Charlie Hanks, Margaret and Andrew Lear, Leslie Mabon, John Malster, Ann Miller, Miranda Montgomery, Bryan Morrison, Joshua Msika, Lorna Patterson, Chris Pepper, Annabel Pinker, Ian Scott, Pat Scott, Christine Steiner, Emma Stewart, Katie Stewart, Andrew Tassell, Leanne Townsend, Nikki and James Yoxall, David Watts, the Grow it, Cook it, Eat it team at BBC Radio Scotland, and everyone at the Scottish Sculpture Workshop.

And finally to Yvonne Billimore, Richard Muscat and Mariuccia Muscat, for all kinds of care, encouragement, sharp-eyes and support throughout.

Town is the Garden Chapbooks: Plants
Published by Deveron Projects and Intellect in 2021

Edited by Joss Allen and Caroline Gatt
Layout by Joss Allen
Cover illustrations by Jamie Johnson
Printed and bound by Footprint Workers Cooperative, Leeds

Typeface: Adobe Casion Pro / Garamond Pro
Paper: Context Natural / Evercopy Plus

ISBN 978-1-907115-37-0

Deveron Projects is a company limited by guarantee, registered in Scotland No. SC391020 and a registered Scottish Charity No. SC024261

Town is the Garden Chapbooks
Deveron Projects and Intellect

Compost
/
Joss Allen and María Puig de la Bellacasa

Compost

Permaculture practices are ethical doings
Maria Puig de la Bellacasa

Town is the Garden compost recipes
Joss Allen

Permaculture practices are ethical doings
Maria Puig de la Bellacasa

A good compost is not just a pile of organic waste...

~ Maria Puig de la Bellacasa, 2017

Permaculture practices are ethical doings that engage with ordinary personal living and subsistence as part of a collective effort that includes non-humans. They decenter human agency without denying its specificity. They promote ethical obligations that do not start from, nor aim at, moral norms but are articulated as existential and concrete necessities. These ethics are born out of material constraints and situated relationalities in the making with other people, living beings, and earth's "resources." Thus, the "principles": care for the earth and people and return of the surplus are both quite generic—their actualizations vary—and involve design principles, that is, very concrete, specific, material, and sometimes inescapable ways to work with patterns of bios (ecological cycles, physical forces). Among people who have followed these trainings, stories abound about their subsequent attempts to implement the practices they learned—in local communities both in urban and rural environments, from a backyard to the local council, or joining larger ways of public eco-activism. Many strongly insist that the trainings and other collective ways of engaging in permaculture

2

have changed their personal everyday ways of relating with food, plants, animals, technologies, and resources, and affected how they valued their own impact on the planet in smaller and bigger ways. Activities can go from starting to compost food waste, to plant and produce food locally, to promote ecological building. But even when actions are acknowledged as deeply intimate or individual—as can be a spiritual connection to a tree, or the building of one's self as a more ecological person—they are affirmed as collective.

The "collective" here does not only include humans but the plants we cultivate, the animals we raise and eat (or rather not), and Earth's energetic resources: air, water. It is in connection with these that human and non- human "individuals" live and act. At every level of human subsistence we depend on them—and in these specific contexts of eco-design painfully aware of ecological disruption—*they* are considered as also depending on us. And as such, humans exist only in a web of living co-vulnerabilities

Permaculture ethics of care are based on the perception that we are embedded in a web of complex relationships in which personal actions have consequences for more than ourselves and our kin. And, conversely, these collective connections transform "our" personal life. The ecological perception of being part of the earth, a part that does its specific share of care, requires Earth not to be a spiritual or visionary image—for example, Gaia—but is felt. Earth as "real dirt under our fingernails" (Starhawk, 2004, 6), and that our bodies are conceived materially as part of it, for example, responding to the needs of water because we *are* water (Lohan, 2008); human energy, including activist energy (Shiva, 2008), being a living material processed by other forms of life. So while permaculture ethical principles can indeed be read as ideas that practitioners become able of transforming into doings, I believe it is more accurate to say that it is the ongoing engagement with personal-collective doings that gradually transforms the way we feel, think, and engage, with principles and ideas. Ongoing doings thicken the meanings of the principles by, for instance, requiring that we learn more in order to know the needs of the soils we take for granted (Ingham, 1999) or other biological and ecological processes, such as the water cycles.

Before continuing, I want to mention a simple example of one of such ethical doings: practicing composting. For people living in urban areas com-

4

posting is a more or less accessible practical technique of caring for the earth, an everyday task of returning the surplus and aiming to produce "no waste" (Carlsson, 2008, 9). It is a relational practice that engages ways of knowing. A good compost is not just a pile of organic waste, and therefore compost techniques are an important part of Earth activist trainings. Not only how to keep a good compost going, but also how to become knowledgeable regarding the liveliness, and needs, of a pile of compost. For instance, one can check if a pile of compost is healthy by attending to the population of pink sticky worms. Worms, in compost—some people keep worm buckets in their kitchens—are a good example of the non-human beings we live with and of which permaculture ethics makes you aware, but not the only one: "anyone who eats should care about the microorganisms in the soil" (Starhawk, 2004, 8). Here naturecultural interdependency is not only more than a moral principle, it is also more than a matter of fact—or technique—that we become aware of. It becomes a matter of care to be involved in through ethical doings.

I am interested in how this "we should care" doesn't work without a transformation of ethos by which obligation emerges within a necessary doing, as well as doings that transform or confirm obligation. I emphasize the word "doing" to mark the ordinariness, the uneventful connotation of this process, in contrast with "action" or distinct moments of decision-making or other ways of delineating ethical events. Obligation toward worms is a good example of doing-obligation. Worms are a more visible manifestation of soil life than microorganisms, but they are as easy to neglect. Caring for the worms is not a given: most people have learned to be disgusted by them. In permaculture trainings they become a signifier of a transformation in feelings as we are invited to appreciate them—"worms are the great creators of fertility. They tunnel into the soil, turning and aerating it. They eat soil particles and rotting food, passing them through their gut and turning them into worm castings, an extremely valuable form of fertilizer, high in nitrogen, minerals and trace elements" (Starhawk, 2004, 170). Becoming able of a caring obligation toward worms as our earthy companions in this messy and muddy way is nurtured by hands on dirt, curiosity, and even love for the needs of an "other," whether this is the people we live with, the animals we care for, or the soil we plant in. It is by working with them, by feeding them and gathering their castings as food for plants, that a relationship is created that acknowledges these interdependencies: while some still might find them disgusting, this is not incompatible with a sense that these neglectible sticky beings appear as quite amazing as well as indispensable—they *take care* of our waste, they process it so that it becomes food again.[1]

This caring obligation is not reducible to "feel good" or "nice feelings"; repulsion is not incompatible with affectionate care (as anybody who has ever changed a baby's soiled diaper or cleaned up the vomit of a sick friend might know). Neither is this obligation to care for an interdependent earthy other understandable as a utilitarian one—I

1. Sociopolitical and affective engagements with earthworms exceed the scientific realms of biology. Filippo Bertoni's work is interesting in this regard (Bertoni 2013; Abrahamsson and Bertoni 2014; see also Clark, York, and Bellamy Foster 2009). Conversely, organizational metaphors are also borrowed by biologists and environmental managers to refer to these soil inhabitants, such as "soil engineers" (Lavelle 2000) or even "soil managers" (Sinha et al. 2011). A constant source of inspiration for those fascinated by earthworms remains Charles Darwin's *The Formation of Vegetable Mould, through the Action of Worms, with Observations on Their Habits* (Darwin 1881).

take care of Earth, via soil and the worms, because I *need* them, because they are of use to me. It is true that some of the teachings of permaculture techniques emphasize that when we don't listen to what nonhumans are saying, experiencing, needing, the responses are consequential for us, too—from the everyday failures and mistakes faced by every grower, to the extinctions and animal-related epidemics among many other failures of care. In contrast, other Earth beings are not discussed as existing to serve "us"—on the contrary, utilitarian approaches are constantly challenged, and the notion that nature provides "services" (see chapter 5[in Puig, 2017]) is not characteristic of permaculture. But if this is not a utilitarian relation, it is not either an altruistic, self-sacrificing one, where nature has value for "itself." While this traditional debate on altruistic versus utilitarian environmental stewardship might be important in other settings (for a discussion of these debates, see Thompson, 1995), here it precludes a speculative engagement with what could be becoming possible in this specific conception of relationships and mutual obligation where living-with rather than living-*on* or living-*for* are at stake.

As I mentioned earlier, human agency in the

permaculture ecosmology is nature working. This means that humans are full participants to the becoming of natural worlds. However, they have their own worldly tasks—their own naturecultural ways of being in this relation. Creating "abundance" by working with nature is affirmed as a typical human skill and contribution. Yet abundance is not considered a surplus of life (as yield) that can be squandered, or as self-regenerative biocapital to invest in a speculative future (Cooper, 2008). On the contrary, it is only by returning the surplus of life— for example, by composting—that the production of abundance can be nurtured. Working-with-nature is something that permaculture activists consider wisdom shared and maintained by alternative agricultural practices that have somehow survived within or in spite of industrialized agriculture, for instance, in the syncretic practices of contemporary indigenous populations. Starhawk cites Mabel McKay, a Powo healer: "When people don't use the plants, they get scarce. You must use them so they will come up again. All plants are like that. If they're not gathered from, or talked to and cared about, they'll die" (quoted in Starhawk, 2004, 9; see also Mendum, 2009). And yet, that human workings in the ecologies we engage with are vital doesn't mean they are at the center. The irony is that it is considered a typical aim of good permaculture to be able to reduce human work as much as possible. In some places, the role of human agency might be to let be. For instance, some plants should be ignored because they are not there for humans, but for others—animals.[2] It could be said that letting other than humans be, a kind of conscious neglect, is also part of the task of care. This points to a hesitation that some beings might be out of reach of care for better or worse or might require a form of ethicality that attaints the limits of embodied relational efforts, as in the case of extinct species that we cannot sense (Yusoff, 2013). What I am seeking here is not to delineate a universally reaching imperative of care that would define human relations with all Earth beings but to specifically learn from these doings of care that in-

2. I want to dearly thank the Grasshawgs, an international, virtually linked group of doctoral students working with Eben Kirksey, for their generous reading of an earlier version of this chapter and chapter 5 and for their inspiring suggestions. In particular here, Karin Bolender suggested how sometimes beings and things can be better off out of the reach of human care.

clude practical, particular, shifting relations where humans are involved with other than humans in ways not reducible to a human-centered-use and are also radically naturecultural.

Once again, my insistence on this naming attempts to short-circuit the reduction of this ethics to one or the other side of humanist binaries. Of course, one could argue that because permaculturists often present the practice as a better "science" it remains within an epistemocentric humanist vision (Holmgren, 2002). But what I have observed in my work with permaculture collectives and permaculture-inspired activism is that humanism and scientism are often advanced somewhat defensively to respond to external identifications of this movement with ecological visions that put "other" beings before humans—for example, considering humans as a separate, destructive, invasive species and science and technology as evil—or that encourage a nostalgic back-to-nature ideal. Beyond this "defensive," or justificatory image (that has nonetheless performative effects in the transformation of permaculture activism in a network of accredited trainings), the accent is rather put on a commitment to the "people" of Earth, inseparably including human and nonhuman beings in a range of different agencies and doings that need each other. Without caring for other beings, we cannot care for humans. Without caring for humans, we cannot care for the ecologies that they live in. Care for "the environment"—as something surrounding "us"—wouldn't be a good way to conceptualize these ethics.

There is another reason why altruist self-erasure or sacrifice (of humans) does not respond better than a utilitarian perspective to these relations. If I read these practices as marked by a form of biopolitical ethics attuned to naturecultural awareness, it is also because here care for one's body-self is not separable from peoplecare and Earthcare. This movement exemplifies well the interdependence of the "three ecologies"—of self (body and psyche), the collective, and the earth—that Félix Guattari famously called upon with political urgency for the near future, believing that none could be realizable without the other (Guattari, 2000). As Starhawk considers, material-spiritual balance cannot be attained through abstract engagement with caring for the earth. On the contrary, the reference to an "ideal" Earth leads "our spiritual, psychic, and physical health" to "become devitalized and deeply unbalanced" (Starhawk, 2004, 6). Conversely, in permaculture trainings there is an insistence on not neglecting the needs of one's body-psyche in the profit of "serving"—burnout is taken into account as a typical activist condition. Thus, while activist care of one's self is embedded in obligation toward a collective, it is not considered "healthy," or effective, to ground care in an altruistic ethics in the face of environmental destruction. As Katie Renz puts it, permaculture is "not some last-ditch effort in the emaciated face of scarcity, but a cultivation of an intimate relationship with one's natural surroundings to create abundance for oneself, for human communities, and the earth" (Renz, 2003). Admittedly, the aim is not modest, or self-sacrificial. It is not even sustainability. It is abundance. In the same way, the affect cultivated in Earth activist trainings is not despondency in the face of the impossible but joy of acting for possibility. In terms of Joan Haran, here hope is a praxis (Haran, 2010).

Ultimately, permaculture ethics is a situated ethics. I am brought back to one of the mottos incessantly repeated in trainings and manuals: "It depends" is the answer to almost every permaculture question. The actualization of principles of caring are always created in an interrelated doing with the needs of a place, a land, a neighborhood, a city, even when a particular action is considered with regard to its extended global connections. Here, "personal" agencies of everyday care are inseparable from their collective ecological significance. It is important to remember that permaculture ethics are not only about planting food or raising animals or sustainable building. In many of its versions, and strongly within the Earth Activist Training tradition, they are also related to public actions of civil disobedience and nonviolent direct action—guerrilla garden creation, public demonstration of techniques in alter-globalization oppositional events, "seedbombing" (Starhawk, 2004, 2002; see interview with Olhsen in Carlsson, 2008, 74–79). More generally, permaculture ethics are thought also as forms of organizing—for instance, promoting forms of collaborative direct democratic sharing instead of competition. They are not about an abstract external vision of the practices of others but an intrinsic transformation of ethos.

We are grateful to Maria Puig de la Bellacasa and the University of Minnesota Press who kindly allowed us to publish this extract from Matters of Care: Speculative Ethics in More Than Human Worlds *(Minneapolis: University of Minnesota Press, 2017),*

145–151. We urge you to seek it out and read the whole thing!

References

Carlsson, Chriss. *Nowtopia: How Pirate Programmers, Outlaw Bicyclists, and Vacant-Lot Gardeners Are Inventing the Future Today!* (Edinburgh: AK Press, 2008).

Cooper, Melinda. *Life as Surplus: Biotechnology and Capitalism in the Neo- liberal Era* (Seattle: University of Washington Press, 2008).

Guattari, Félix. *The Three Ecologies* (London: Athlone, 2000).

Holmgren, David. *Permaculture: Principles and Pathways Beyond Sustainability* (Hepburn, Victoria: Holmgren Design Services, 2002).

Ingham, Elaine. *The Compost Tea Brewing Manual*, 5th ed. (Bentley: Soil Foodweb Institute, 2002).

Mendum, Ruth. "Subjectivity and Plant Domestication: Decoding the Agency of Vegetable Food Crops." *Subjectivity* 28 (2009). 316–33.

Renz, Katie. "Cultivating Hope at Earth Activist Training". *Hopedance* 39 (2003).

Shiva, Vandana. *Soil Not Oil: Environmental Jus-*

tice in a Time of Climate Crisis (Cambridge, Mass.: South End Press, 2008).

Starhawk. *The Earth Path: Grounding Your Spirit in the Rhythms of Nature* (San Francisco: Harper Collins, 2004).

Thompson, Paul B. *The Spirit of the Soil: Agriculture and Environmental Ethics* (New York: Routledge, 1995).

Yusoff, Kathryn. "Insensible Worlds: Postrelational Ethics, Indeterminacy, and the (K)nots of Relating". *Environment and Planning D: Society and Space* 31:2 (2008). 208–26.

18

19

Town is the Garden compost recipes
Joss Allen

Get involved. Become a citizen of decomposition. Fall in love with mesophiles. Get down with the earthworms!

~ Joss Allen, this volume

Composting is a wonder. As Jennifer Mae Hamilton and Astrida Niemanis say, compost is "a multi-species wonderland."[1] An incredible heap full of vitality and possibility!

Everyone at Deveron Projects takes part in composting. It is embedded into the weekly routines of the office. Communal Friday lunches are followed by cleaning the kitchen, separating out the food waste and taking out the compost bin. For the Town is the Garden project it was a good place to begin thinking about soil care, food waste and

1. See https://compostingfeminisms.wordpress.com/about/.

composting, from the office outwards. One of the first things the Town is the Garden team did was to upgrade Deveron Projects' composting site from a dilapidated pile of rotten pallets, planks and tarps to a more substantial system of four large wooden bays. We wanted to think more deeply about composting. To think of composting not only as an office practice but as relational and as a part of an ethics of care that extends beyond the human. As Maria Puig de la Bellacasa says "a good compost is not just a pile of organic waste" (2017, 146). Our new compost bays became a place to practice thinking and doing ecology, otherwise.

We were not instinctively "good composters" and we often struggled to translate our enthusiasm into action in the community. We certainly made plenty of mistakes but we learned a lot through the process—one summer our compost bays attracted so many flies nobody wanted to take out and empty the office compost bin for weeks. The recipes that follow are an attempt to capture some of that learning, from our mistakes and our successes. We hope you find them useful.

Composting can be done on almost any scale, but generally larger heaps will create better conditions for decomposition. If you don't have space or access to a site where you can compost, perhaps your neighbours already compost and you could add in to theirs. Or maybe between a group of houses a communal compost site could be started. You can even try composting in your house by developing a small vermicomposting system (working with worms) or through bokashi (fermenting with special bacteria). You could try out composting as a metaphor in all sorts of situations too...

To quote ecosexual artists Beth Stephens and Annie Sprinkle, "Composting is so hot!" The Town is the Garden team certainly think so. Get involved. Become a citizen of decomposition. Fall in love with mesophiles. Get down with the earthworms!

Cold Compost Recipe

Choose the right site. Ideally, you want it to be somewhere that is not going to get too hot or too wet. A slightly shady spot would be best. Your wee pals, the microorganisms that are going to be doing all the work breaking the compost down, prefer consistent conditions. The heap is best situated on bare earth as well, this allows all the worms and other organisms to aerate the heap. Also think about what you will be doing with the compost afterwards: if you can avoid having to transport the compost far, all the better. We had ours fairly close to the office front door (so you didn't have to take the kitchen scraps too far, an incentive to get people to do it!), and close to our greenhouse (where we used the compost for seedlings and potting up).

You will need:

A large container for your compost: You can build a simple compost bay system using old pallets to create the back and sides. Ideally, each bay should be at least 1m³. Minimum of two bays is best (one being filled, one composting). We found that wooden compost heaps like this reduced the need for turning. The recipe also works for other types of compost bins.

Brown material (carbon rich): deciduous leaves, hedge clippings, twiggy prunings / stems, shredded cardboard / egg boxes, shredded newspaper, straw.

Green material (nitrogen rich): grass cuttings, vegetable peelings, rotten fruit and other uncooked kitchen scraps, seedling thinings, spent annual plants, plant tops (without roots and seed heads), seaweed.

Water or some lovely smelly liquid of some kind, such as: urine or weed tea*.

Optional: Lime (ground limestone or calcified seaweed) or potash (ashes from a fire)**; manure (cow, horse or chicken); old carpets (wool is best) and/or tarpaulin for covering.

Method:

Place thin twigs, stems or straw on the bottom layer of the heap. This will help to encourage air circulation. Start to layer the heap with the different materials, alternating between the brown and the green, wet and dry. If you have it, add in some manure. This will help activate the heap.

It's important to keep the compost moist (but not sodden or soaking!), so give your heap a good water. Adding urine or weed tea can help boost the compost. Cover the heap. Use whatever you have at hand. We used old wool carpets and tarpaulins. Covering it helps keep in moisture and heat.

It is best to make your heap in as little steps as possible, ideally filling it up in one go (see hot composting recipe). But this isn't always practical. We generally started our heaps off about ¼ to ⅓ to begin with, then tried to keep a good mix of materials as we filled it up over several weeks. For best results, you need to try and stick to a ratio of about one-third green material to two-thirds brown material, so more carbon than nitrogen. It's the brown materials that help oxygen to penetrate the heap, nourishing the lovely micro-organisms living in there. Too much of the green stuff can lead to anaerobic (lack of oxygen) decomposing , where the heap becomes dense and smelly, and slows right down. When adding in green stuff like food scraps it's important to cover them, either with a layer of brown stuff or even a small amount of compost— this can also help introduce more microorganism to the heap. Mixing the green stuff with the layer below also helps. Exposed green stuff will smell and attract a lot of flies, so keep it covered. If in doubt, add more brown stuff!

Turn the heap. This helps to aerate it, adding in more oxygen and "cooking" the compost quicker. This can be a bit of a job but you can do it as you go along, avoiding the need to turn the whole lot at a time. Mixing up the layers with a fork or spade every time you add in more material can really help to keep it aerated. The need for turning can also be avoided if you keep your heap well aerated by adding in plenty of course material like straw and using some kind of container with fairly open sides, such as one built from pallets or chicken wire.

Once we had emptied one of our compost bays of compost, we would often then turn the bay next to it into the empty one—doing this maybe four times a year. This was a good opportunity to see what was happening in the heap, to check its health and whether it was ready or not. It is ready when the majority of the material has broken down and you're left with a dark brown compost with a crumbly soil-like texture; it should smell like a lovely damp wood. Bits that haven't fully broken down can be riddled (sieved) out and put back into the compost bay. Riddling compost is a bit like a crude kind of archaeology; you'd be amazed at what turned up in our compost heap!

Hot Compost Recipe

Hot composting is a good way to compost a lot of material all at once, but there can be a little bit more preparation and care involved. For it to work best, you will need all the material to be cut-up or shredded to a fairly small size before you start. Hot composting is a good group activity, get your pals/neighbours involved and make a day of it.

You will need:

Roughly equal quantities of brown and green material (see Cold Compost Recipe above)—for a first attempt, mixing grass cuttings and leaves works well. Plus: a tarpaulin or old carpet (to cover the heap); a fork of shovel for turning; thermometer; a shovel full of compost, manure or soil; a bin or container (optional).

Method:

Mix the materials together and build a heap roughly 1m^2 and piled 1m high—or if using a container, fill the container full. Add in the shovel full of compost/manure/soil, this helps kickstart the process, adding in lots of microorganisms that'll help do the work.

Water the heap as you go, it should be damp but not sodden.

Cover your heap with a tarpaulin or bit of old carpet. Record its daily temperature, the heap should get up to somewhere between 49 and 80°C after about five days.

When the heap begins to cool, dropping below 43°C, after about seven to ten days, it is time to turn it. Turn the outside edges into the middle and bring the inside material to the outside. Cover your heap and leave for another seven to ten days.

Repeat this cycle (turning when cool) for approx. one to two months, or until you find it is no longer heating up.

Then leave covered for a couple of weeks to finish "curing" (to make sure the microorganisms have finished their work), then it is ready to use.[2] By this point the heap should have really transformed. You are looking for a dark crumbly soil-like consistency with that wonderful damp woodland smell.

Note: times can really vary depending on how the heap was built and outside temperatures. In the cold northeast of Scotland in reality sometimes it took closer to four months for the compost to be

2. If you are not sure, take a handful of compost and place in a reusable sealed plastic bag, after three days it should still smell lovely and earthy. If it smells sour, the microorganism are still at work and need some more time.

30

ready to use.

Hugel Heap Recipe

Hugel heaps, or hugelkultur to give them their proper name, are a kind of raised bed built on rotten wood, with branches, leaves, straw and compost piled on top. A sort of compost heap you plant directly into. The wood retains water, and as it breaks down, slowly releases heat and nutrients. The idea is to create a raised bed which needs minimal watering or feeding. Hugel heaps can last up to twenty years with very little input (or so we've heard). It's a really smart way of harnessing the powers of decay and decomposition.

We looked into building hugel heaps on public land, using garden waste which was already being dumped nearby and green waste from the council (branches and grass cuttings), which they were desperate to get rid of. We thought these could then be planted with a range of edibles and pollinators, such as soft fruits and berries. We made a few test heaps for the local council, as examples, but they are yet to take to the idea…

Before you begin, think about what you plan to grow in your heap (some ideas below), how much material you have to build it, and what kind of size will be manageable for you. Just be conscious of the fact that the rotting wood will initially draw in nitrogen as it decomposes, so this needs to be compensated with enough nitrogen rich material and/or initially planted with nitrogen fixing crops such as legumes or plants which require minimal nitrogen.

You will need:

Logs of various sizes and kinds (ideally partially rotted), large ones for the very bottom of the heap. A mixture of hard and soft wood is best. Try to avoid having too many logs from coniferous trees and any other type of tree that might have anti-microbial/fungal properties or which are particularly resistant to decay. Plus: Branches, brush, twigs, woody stems, etc.; a mixture of other brown material such as leaves, straw, and hedge clippings; a mixture of green materials such as grass cuttings and seaweed; aged manure; compost or topsoil.

Method:

Remove turf from site, keep nearby. Dig a trench

your desired size. It needs to be at least 30cm deep.

Place the largest logs in the bottom of the trench, then layer up going from biggest to smallest. Try also to keep hardwoods on the bottom and softwoods on top. Less rotted wood is best put near the bottom of the pile too. Softwoods will decompose faster, giving of more nutrients first, they will also draw in nitrogen to begin with. This is why you need plenty of nitrogen rich stuff on top.

On top of the logs lay the cut turf, grass side down.

Then start to layer it up with a mixture of manure, brown and green materials. The heaps can be any height but it is best to make them as tall as possible (up to 1.8m is recommended) and with steep sides. This means you have more growing space (surface area) and the better they are at retaining moisture (greater mass). In reality, we often only managed to make ours about 1m tall.

Finally add a layer of compost or topsoil, 5–10cm. Then add a layer of mulch, such as some more straw. Now you are ready to plant it up.

What to plant in a heap:

Hugel heaps can be planted with a range of annuals, biannuals and perennials mixed together, but it is important to think about where you plant them in the heap. As the heap decomposes over time it will begin to slowly decrease in height, this means that the top section in particular (the hump of the heap) could start to develop air pockets under the top layer of soil. So, planting a tree for instance on top of the pile might not be such a good idea. Avoiding root crops, at least in the first few years, is also probably a good idea. Here are a few things we considered planting in ours:

Crops grown for just one year (annuals/biennials): courgettes, marrows and squashes; salads and lettuces; spinach and chard; herbs, such as parsley or coriander;

Crops grown continuously (perennials): strawberries; alliums, such as chives; fruit bushes, such as raspberries or blackcurrants; rhubarb; herbs, such as sage or mint.

It doesn't just have to be edible crops either, think about medicinal/other herbal plants you might use; and of course, plants that help support other creatures such as pollinating insects like bees.

34

Alternatives: Hugelkultur can be used on all sorts of scales. You could use it as a technique for filling containers and small raised beds, adjusting the size of logs used, or make giant 2m+ heaps by burying really big logs and using repurposed wooden pallets for sides. In some of our raised beds we adopted a "lasagne" style approach, layering up materials (minus the logs) with a good layer of compost on top.

* Weed tea

We were always a little confused about what to do with perennial or so-called "pernicious" weeds. Until Lindy (project gardener) came on the idea of putting them (seeds removed) in a large container and filling it with water and leaving them for a week or so to rot. The lovely smelly liquid could be diluted and used to feed the garden, as well as being added to the compost heap to keep it moist. The rotted plants could then be added as a layer to a hot compost heap.

** Weed potash

Another good method for dealing with perennial

weeds is to burn them and then add the ash into the compost as a nutrient rich type potash.

Some plants might survive being cold or hot composted, or being left to rot in water, and some seeds might even survive being burned, so you still need to be a bit careful.

A note on weeds

In "dealing with weeds", our approach has been to try and shift how we think about them: to make space for weeds, to think with them rather than plotting their eradication.[3] To appreciate them in broader ecological sense, in both the garden and in landscapes beyond. What might weeds teach us for example about soil and climatic conditions, about human-disturbances in the land? What might we

3. Of course, sometimes you just need to do some weeding. In our experience, one of the best methods for reducing the amount of weeding you have to do (and the amount of digging) in the garden is to adopt a "no dig" approach, where you try to avoid disturbing the structure of the soil through cultivation, instead working with mulching and other methods to add organic matter directly on top. Building soil structure up, rather than digging down into it. For no dig guidance, we suggest turning to Charles Dowding (https://charlesdowding.co.uk/).

learn from their histories and stories about more-than-human world making? What kinds of nutritional benefits might they offer us humans (as well as the compost heap)?—if you can't compost them maybe you can eat them, check out Eleanor Brown's essay, "Foraging, an incidental mindfulness practice", in *Plants* as part of this collection for some ideas. But also to try to appreciate them beyond relationships based purely on utility (or inutility), towards those of appreciation, even reciprocity. How might we collaborate *with* weeds?[4]

4. A few resources to get you started thinking with weeds: Anna Lawrence, "To Be a Weed", *The Ethnobotanical Assembly,* 4 (2019), https://www.tea-assembly.com/issues/2019/9/29/to-be-a-weed; Richard Mabey, *Weeds: How Vagabond Plants Gatecrashed Civilisation and Changed the Way We Think About Nature* (Profile, 2012); Anna Tsing, "The Buck, the Bull, and the Dream of the Stag: Some unexpected weeds of the Anthropocene" *Suomen Antropologi: Journal of the Finnish Anthropological Society, 42*:1 (2017), https://journal.fi/suomenantropologi/article/view/65084.

Further resources

Ball, Bruce C. *The Landscape Below: Soil, soul and agriculture* (UK: Wild Goose Publications, 2015).

Hills, Lawrence D. *Organic Gardening* (UK: Penguin, 1977).

Gershuny, Grace., and Smillie, Joseph. *The Soul of Soil: A Soil-Building Guide for Master Gardeners and Farmers, 4th edition* (Vermount; Chelsea Green, 1999).

Holmgren, David. *Permaculture: Principles & Pathways Beyond Sustainability* (UK: Permanent Publications, 2011).

Holzer, Sepp. *Permaculture: A Practical Guide for Farmers, Smallholders and Gardeners* (UK: Permanent Publications, 2010).

Lawrence, Anna. "To Be a Weed". *The Ethnobotanical Assembly*, 4 (2019). Accessed online. https://www.tea-assembly.com/issues/2019/9/29/to-be-a-weed

Logan, William Bryant. *Dirt: The Ecstatic Skin of the Earth* (USA: W.W. Norton & Company; reprint edition, 2007).

Louie, Rebecca. *Compost City: Practical Composting Know-How for Small-Space Living* (Boulder: Roost Books, 2015).

Lyons, Kristina M. *Vital Decomposition: Soil practitioners and life politics.* (Durham: Duke University Press, 2020).

Mabey, Richard. *Weeds: How Vagabond Plants Gatecrashed Civilisation and Changed the Way We Think About Nature* (UK: Profile, 2012).

Marting, Deborah L., and Gershuny, Grace (eds.). *The Roasdale Book of Composting: Easy Methods for Every Gardener* (USA: Rodale Books, revised an updated edition, 2018).

Shapiro, Howard-Yana., and Harrisson, John. *Gardening for the Future of the Earth* (USA: Bantam Doubleday Dell, 2000).

Shiva, Vandana. *Soil not Oil: Environmental Jus-*

tice in an Age of Climate Crisis (Boston: South End Press, 2008).

Tsing, Ann. "The Buck, the Bull, and the Dream of the Stag: Some unexpected weeds of the Anthropocene". *Suomen Antropologi: Journal of the Finnish Anthropological Society*, *42*:1 (2017). Accessed online. https://journal.fi/suomenantropologi/article/view/65084

Whitefield, Patrick. *The Earth Care Manual* (UK: Permanent Publications, 2004).

Online resources:

Permaculture Magazine. "How to make a hugelkultur bed" [video]. https://www.permaculture.co.uk/videos/how-make-hugelkultur-bed

Richards. Huw. "The Art of Lazy Composting: How to Make High-Quality Compost the Simple Way" [video]. *Youtube* (2020). https://www.youtube.com/watch?v=swLkA1cHJ4Y

Joss Allen can be found at the edges of the garden, amongst the weeds and compost heaps. He is an art-worker and gardener exploring how creative practices can shape earthy politics, community economies and ecological ways of being in playful, radical, responsive and meaningful ways.

Maria Puig de la Bellacasa currently works at the Centre for Interdisciplinary Methodologies, University of Warwick. Her work is interdisciplinary, working with science and technology studies, cultural geographies, feminist theory, the environmental humanities and political ecology. She is interested in how questions of ethics, politics and justice affect and are affected by scientific practices, as well as on the socio-cultural imaginaries enacted by technoscientific intervention.

Town is the Garden

A community food growing project, *of sorts*.

For three years the Town is the Garden team could be found at the margins of the garden. Amongst the weeds and compost heaps, they explored what it might mean to *think with* the garden. Through crafting gardens, vegetable plots and orchards they attempted to rethink how a community might feed itself as it faces up to the global climate and ecological emergency. Through the processes of learning and sharing skills in relation to growing food, from planting seeds to preserving the harvest, they asked how we might also begin to pay better attention to the entanglement of human and more-than-human worlds. They asked how might the garden be a site of both resistance and resilience? A place for *thinking* and *doing* ecology, otherwise.

This is *Compost* in a collection of seven chapbooks by the *Town is the Garden* that attempt to capture some of the diverse ways of thinking, doing and knowing the project explored with some of the people they explored them with. It includes contributions from Eleanor Brown and Alexandra Falter (*Plants*), Jonathan Baxter & Sarah Gittins (*Orchard*), Joe Crowdy (*Garden*), Dawn Finch

44

(*Seeds*), Maria Puig de la Bellacasa (*Compost*), and Joss Allen, Caroline Gatt and Elisabetta Rattalino (*Story*). With cover illustrations by Jamie Johnson.

The Town is the Garden team included: Joss Allen (2017–20), Rhian Davies (2019–20), Caroline Gatt (2018–20), Camille Sineau (2017–18), and Lindy Young (2017–19).

https://www.deveron-projects.com/town-garden

The *Town is the Garden* team would like to thank everyone who contributed to these chapbooks and Footprint Workers Cooperative for their exceptional printing skills.

A massive thank you to everyone at Deveron Projects, staff, board and interns (too many to name), especially Petra Pennington, Robyn Wolsey and Claudia Zeiske—for their support and guidance—and the Neep & Okra Kitchen team— with whom we latterly shared space and ideas with. To Alex Severn, our wonderful intern, on a student placement from the University of Aberdeen. To our generous funders Aberdeenshire Council, Action Earth, Climate Challenge Fund, Community Growing Fund, Creative Scotland, Finnis Scott Foundation, Groundwork, and Grow Wild. Many thanks to the Aberdeenshire Environmental

Forum for awarding the Green Butterfly Award to Huntly Town, partly in recognition of the work of the *Town is the Garden* project. The award gave the team great encouragement.

We would like to thank everyone who took part in the *Town is the Garden* project, for their generosity, patience and support. In particular those who contributed to the programme: Matt Aitkenhead, Andy Smith, Charlie Ashton, Grace Banks, Rosa Bevan and James Reid, John Bolland, Stephen Brandes, Alan Carter, Karen Collins, Doug Cookson, Uist Corrigan, Bob Donald, David Easton and Jane Lockyer, Petra/Patrick Geddes, Katrina Flad, Marguerite Fleming, Vicky Flood, David Foubister, Cristina Grasseni, Charlie Hanks, Margaret and Andrew Lear, Leslie Mabon, John Malster, Ann Miller, Miranda Montgomery, Bryan Morrison, Joshua Msika, Lorna Patterson, Chris Pepper, Annabel Pinker, Ian Scott, Pat Scott, Christine Steiner, Emma Stewart, Katie Stewart, Andrew Tassell, Leanne Townsend, Nikki and James Yoxall, David Watts, the Grow it, Cook it, Eat it team at BBC Radio Scotland, and everyone at the Scottish Sculpture Workshop.

And finally to Yvonne Billimore, Richard Muscat and Mariuccia Muscat, for all kinds of care, encouragement, sharp-eyes and support throughout.

Town is the Garden Chapbooks: Compost
Published by Deveron Projects and Intellect in 2021

Edited by Joss Allen and Caroline Gatt
Layout by Joss Allen
Cover illustrations by Jamie Johnson
Printed and bound by Footprint Workers Cooperative, Leeds

Typeface: Adobe Casion Pro / Garamond Pro
Paper: Context Natural / Evercopy Plus

ISBN 978-1-907115-37-0

Deveron Projects is a company limited by guarantee, registered in Scotland No. SC391020 and a registered Scottish Charity No. SC024261

Town is the Garden Chapbooks
Deveron Projects and Intellect

Orchard

/

Joss Allen, Jonathan Baxter and Sarah Gittins

Orchard

*Future Fruit: Rethinking Huntly
from a Geddesian perspective*
Jonathan Baxter & Sarah Gittins

Huntly Orchard tea recipe
Joss Allen

*Future Fruit: Rethinking Huntly
from a Geddesian perspective*
Jonathan Baxter & Sarah Gittins

Illustrations

Figure 1: *Cosmic Walk with Patrick (Petra) Geddes*
Figure 2: *More-than-human (grafting workshop)*
Figure 3: *Huntly Food Assembly*
Figure 4: *"Notice the living twig... mothering its bud for the next year" (Patrick Geddes) (screen print workshop)*
Figure 6: *Leap - a perspective from the Outlook Tower*
Figure 7: *Arbor Saeculorum (pruning workshop)*
Figure 8: *Orchard tentacular (Fiona running)*
Figure 9: *Exploring the multi-species commons*

What political ecologies do we want to perform? And how might [we] respond to the climate and ecological crisis by learning to care for an orchard?

~ Jonathan Baxter & Sarah Gittins,
this volume

> Like flower and butterfly, city and citizen
> are bound in an abiding partnership of
> mutual aid.
>
> (Geddes in Welter, 2002, 31–32)

This essay has two overlapping aims. To introduce a socially engaged art project undertaken by Jonathan Baxter and Sarah Gittins for Deveron Projects' *Town is the Garden* and to consider the relevance of the Scottish generalist thinker and town planner, Patrick Geddes (1854–1932) for socially engaged art. In this essay, we tell the story of *Future Fruit: Rethinking Huntly from a Geddesian Perspective* (2019–20) and draw attention to a wider set of problems that coalesce around the climate and ecological crisis.[1]

---

1. As a point of clarity, it's worth noting the division of labour this essay performs. Jonathan has written the text and Sarah has drawn the images. In reality this performance is collaborative; a braid of mutual aid.

Collective enquiry

Future Fruit, like all art projects, has a history. It's the history of a collective enquiry. It follows an invitation in 2018 from Joss Allen (Green Coordinator of Deveron Projects' *Town is the Garden*) to begin a conversation about Huntly's community orchard. The invitation picked up a thread from 2010 when Allen joined a Reading Towards Action group organised by D-AiR (Dundee Artists in Residence). Reading Towards Action explored texts relating to art, ecology and social practice and was partly inspired by a project called PRAKTIKA, an event and publication organised by Deveron Arts in 2008.[2] Alongside other Reading Towards Action participants, Allen was particularly interested in Temporary

2. PRAKTIKA taught me two things, both of which I practice in this essay: the need to differentiate between socially engaged art practices (Gibson and Harding in Zeiske, 2008, 2); and the importance of "hospitable criticality" when considering those practices (Sacramento in Zeiske, 4–9). Here, as elsewhere, I follow Sacramento's shadow curatorial lead by "go[ing] beyond a straightforward chronicle of [events] and into more discursive territory" (Zeiske, 4).

Autonomous Zones, Sarah, who was also in the group, was interested in print-based environmental storytelling, and I, as artist-curator, was exploring the generative tension between social and deep ecology. Over time, these and other interests led Allen to *Town is the Garden* and Sarah and I to DUO (Dundee Urban Orchard)—a project that reimagined Dundee through the metaphor of an orchard.[3]

It's from the overlap of these interests that *Future Fruit* took root. First as an invitation to help *Town is the Garden* think through the potential of Huntly's community orchard. Then as an invitation to take up a residency. This involved a research trip to Huntly in February 2019, a residency in August, and a further series of workshops and events from September 2019 to March 2020. During this time, other players entered the scene. And by "players", I really mean, *actants*: an intervenor or operator "which, by virtue of its particular location in an assemblage and the fortuity of being in the right place at the right time makes the difference, makes things happen, becomes the decisive force

3. For more information on DUO, see https://www. dundeeurbanorchard.net.

catalysing the event" (Bennett, 2010, 9).[4]

Here, to be clear, the orchard was an actant. As were the people we met in Huntly—in person and in the wider context of our research. So too was Huntly in its evolution-involution from a once-bustling market town to what now, increasingly, resembles an empty theatre set.

Getting to know you

So, what did *Future Fruit* do when the project became an actant? The first thing we did was stroll through Huntly to visit the community orchard. On that stroll, we noticed that the majority of front gardens were either paved over for parking space or minimally maintained. There were exceptions, and those exceptions mostly related to larger properties, but cared for gardens were not the norm. On further enquiry, when talking to Huntly residents, this impression was confirmed. People were time-

---

4. The term "actant" was coined by Bruno Latour to describe a source of action that "can be human or not, or, most likely, a combination of both" (Bennett, 2010, 9). In what follows I lean heavily on Jane Bennett's use of the term as it relates to her understanding of a materialist political ecology.

4

pressed. And during periods of leisure, people were more likely to leave town than stay at home and care for a garden.

Having arrived at the community orchard, we were struck by two things: the setting of the orchard—a flood plain, formerly farmland, now known as the Meadows—and the orchard's apparent lack of maintenance and care. Regarding the latter, a number of trees were ring-barked (dying or dead), branches and trunks were snapped, no signage or interpretation was visible, a fence surrounding one of the orchards had collapsed, and the two closest benches were broken. Written as a list of negatives, this sounds worse than it was. Superficial damage was our verdict. From this, we surmised that the community orchard was latent, not active. An interpretation based on the "commoning" principle that for an orchard to be a *community* orchard three things have to be in place:

fruit trees, people, and social practices (Bollier, 2014, 15). In Huntly there were fruit and nut trees: apple, pear, plum, damson, and hazelnut. But on our first visit there was no evidence of *sustained* community engagement. Thus, we reasoned, while there was certainly an orchard—a technical term to describe the planting of five or more fruit trees— there wasn't a *community* orchard. This because there wasn't a *human* community engaged in its ongoing maintenance and care.

In contrast to the town's community orchard and front gardens, the energy of Deveron Projects and *Town is the Garden* staff was alive and kicking. No seasonal downtime here. This contrasted with the energy we often encountered when talking to Huntly residents, including representatives of the main organisation responsible for planting the community orchard.[5] This isn't to say that residents of Huntly were downbeat. But there was a sense of strain. People were time-pressed *and* cash-pressed. Indeed, this was one of the reasons

> 5. The existing orchard is made up of two orchard plantings. One by the artist Norma Hunter, through her project, *Bite on the Side*. The other, more extensive orchard, by Huntly-based Networks of Wellbeing.

given for the relative neglect of the orchard: it was planted with the best of intentions, the process had been inclusive and rewarding, but there were no funds for ongoing maintenance and care. As a consequence, the orchard had, for the most part, been left to care for itself.

This question of care is key to thinking about orchards. Especially if your primary concern is the health of the orchard and the work orchards can do to coalesce a public. Here I have in mind Jane Bennett's (2010) claim that we need

> to devise new procedures, technologies, and regimes of perception that enable us to consult nonhumans more closely, or to listen and respond more carefully to their outbreaks, objections, testimonies, and propositions. For these offerings are profoundly important to the health of the political ecologies to which *we* belong (Ibid., 108).

This gets to the heart of *Future Fruit*. It asks—or rather, the orchard might ask—what sort of world do we want to inhabit? What political ecologies do we want to perform? And how might Huntly respond to the climate and ecological crisis by learning to care for an orchard?

If this line of enquiry sounds hyperbolic, perhaps it's because the depth of the question and the possibilities it opens up have become alien to what we now expect from a community orchard. However, the history of community orchards suggests otherwise. In one history at least, community orchards perform a different sort of politics, where the *polis*—originally the City but here glossed as *any* forum for democratic politics—is reimagined as an "open-air community hall" where we can "relax, play, work and learn" together, "enlivened by nature" to "gain knowledge about where our food comes from", learn to grow our food again, "improve our diet", enjoy seasonal festivities, and face up to the multiple challenges of climate change (King and Clifford, 2008, 7).

Of course, community orchards are not the only vehicle to reimagine the *polis*. Any relationship deeply entered into offers opportunities to engage democratic life. But community orchards—even latent community orchards—are readymade vehicles. Or as Geddes might say, a readymade *thinking machine*. They open up a line of flight for rethinking our ecological sensibility by offering a model of the good life that both challenges the bifurcation of human and more-than-human worlds—what Jacques Rancière (2004) would call a partition of the sensible—whilst countering the dominant trend of free market capitalism and the wrecking ball of neoliberalism. A wrecking ball that collapses local economies, degrades local environments and weakens community resilience.

As an example of the latter, I offer Huntly's ongoing challenge of what happens when you allow two supermarkets to be built on the edge of a small market town. Spoiler: the majority of town centre shops close down, people become dependent on the supermarkets for employment and food, and the quality of life dwindles because the comparison—or more specifically, the memory of an alternative—is erased. Or if the comparison remains available—for example, for those who can afford to buy locally grown organic food direct from a producer—it's not there for everyone. And *everyone* is who (and what) community orchards potentially invite.

Knowing what we know

So, if this is one experience a community orchard might offer—an alternative model of the good life, a way to rethink the *polis*—how did *Future Fruit* engage this sensibility? To answer this question, I need to acknowledge the difference between the intention of *Future Fruit* and its outcome. *Future Fruit* was planned for a two-year engagement cycle: to observe and tend the orchard whilst building up a community of orchard volunteers. These orchard volunteers—otherwise known as MCs (Maintenance and Care artists)—would be trained in grafting, pruning, harvesting, and preserving. They would also be encouraged to develop seasonal rites for the orchard; to become orchard *celebrants*—people who recognised the intrinsic value of the orchard and were keen to share this value with others.

This latter emphasis had the intention of moving *Future Fruit* from utility to mutuality; from the merely human use of an orchard—the orchard as object—to understanding the orchard as subject—where the orchard *speaks back*. And this, of course, is one of the central challenges we face as a human community: how to move from

10

an anthropocentric or capitalocentric worldview (a perspective dominated by human and/or capitalist interests) to a worldview that recognises the intrinsic value of the more-than-human world—a world of "things, objects, other animals, living beings, organisms, physical forces, spiritual entities, and humans" (Puig de la Bellacasa, 2017, 1).

One way to do this is to develop social, environmental and economic practices that foster critical forms of reconnection. i.e. practices that *re*-cognise the nature-culture dyad to be a complex system of differing potentialities all with equal—and therefore, *contested*—value. To do this *Future Fruit* rethought Geddes's understanding of the evolution of cities through a practice of "evolutionary remembering".[6] A practice elaborated by John Seed (2007) as follows:

> If we wish to reunite with nature, the first requirement is that we have the intention to re-establish this contact. We are descended from thousands of

6. Geddes wrote extensively on the evolution of cities. A key text being, *Cities in Evolution: An Introduction to the Town Planning Movement and to the Study of Civics* (1915).

human generations who practiced rituals acknowledging our interconnection. Once we get the intention to end the separation we have created, the desired results come naturally from rituals that feel authentic to us. As some are already doing, we can begin to reclaim ancient rituals at the solstices and equinoxes affirming our connections to the changing cycles of the seasons. New rituals—enactments of our intentions— are open to all of us, regardless of our original traditions (Ibid., 13–14).

I'll return to how *Future Fruit* sought to cultivate evolutionary remembering in my discussion of *Aeons and Apple Trees* below. But first I want to draw attention to Seed's emphasis on "rituals that feel authentic to us". This isn't an argument for the *imposition* of ritual. Nor is it an argument for a religious versus secular worldview—albeit that's an argument worth exploring.[7] Instead, it's an

---

7. The argument might be summarised as follows: "without the language game of religion—of God—we lose the relevant possibilities of life with the *meta*ethical self, that uncanny gap/protrusion that troubles every 'technique' of the self" (Santner, 2001, 92).

argument for *ecological* deliberation. For listening to what an orchard (or any other ecology) might have to teach us.

A useful analogy for how this might benefit human beings is given in Richard Mabey's (2006) account of what he calls the "nature cure". A way of asking the questions: "Where do I belong? What's my role? How, in social, emotional, ecological terms, do I find a way of *fitting*?" (Ibid., 10). When Mabey asked these questions in response to his experience of depression, he discovered that what healed him was *not* the experience of *submitting* to nature but "almost the exact opposite process, a sense of being taken not out of myself but back *in*, of nature entering me, firing up the wild bits of my imagination" (Ibid., 224). This is the role that *Future Fruit* imagined the community orchard might play for Huntly: it could fire up the wild bits of our collective imagination and *re-graft* place and folk through practices of evolutionary remembering.

In developing this argument *Future Fruit* drew on Geddes's triadic understanding of place-work-folk. An analytic concept Geddes adapted from the work of Frédéric Le Pay. Geddes used this concept to describe the symbiotic construction of nature

13

and culture in the context of human settlements. In *Future Fruit*'s reading, emphasis was placed on the middle term, "work", and translated through the practice-based metaphor of "grafting"; specifically, the grafting of a chosen scion onto a chosen rootstock.[8] Key to *Future Fruit*'s thinking was the *synthetic* nature of grafting, where that which is *not* one, *becomes* one, whilst retaining the potential to become *something else*. Or to quote Geddes: "From these three separate notes of life we thus get a central unified Chord of Life, with its minor chords as well" (Geddes in Boardman, 1978, 470).

In developing this metaphor, *Future Fruit* emphasised a *radical* reading of Geddes, one that acknowledges the tension between cooperation and competition. In relation to this tension Geddes takes sides. He sides with Peter Kropotkin ([1902] 2006) (an anarchist colleague and friend) in favour of mutual aid—but he doesn't down play the reality of mutual struggle. Hence Geddes's

8. A scion is a branch that determines the variety of fruit. A rootstock is the root system that determines the size of the tree. Within a Geddesian re-reading, scion can be read as "future intention" and rootstock can be read as "place" (geographic location) "place-folk" (natives or neighbours) and "folk-place" (occupations).

well known statement, "[b]y leaves we live" is no mere ecological bromide. It's part of a wider, poetic critique of unfettered capitalism.

> How many people think twice about a leaf? Yet the leaf is the chief product and phenomenon of Life: this is a green world, with animals comparatively few and small, and all dependent upon the leaves. By leaves we live. Some people have strange ideas that they live by money. They think energy is generated by the circulation of coins. But the world is mainly a vast leaf-colony, growing on and forming a leafy soil, not a mere mineral mass: and we live not by the jingling of our coins, but by the fullness of our harvests.[9]

This tension matters when we consider Geddes's understanding of synthesis—"the

9. Quotation from Geddes's 1919 farewell lecture to his students at University College Dundee. See https://www.murdomacdonald.wordpress.com/patrick-geddes-farewell-lecture-to-his-dundee-students-1919. From here on reference to this lecture is noted as "Farewell lecture".

16

intellectual power of comparing and synthesising different ideas" (Macdonald, 2020, 97)—because without this tension Geddes can be read as a mere organicist; someone who downplays the *struggle of history*. While this idealised tendency is clearly marked in Geddes's prose, a radical (and self-critical) reading of Geddes acknowledges this tension.[10] Take, for example, Geddes's "The Notation of Life" diagram; a diagram-as-thinking machine that draws attention to the *difference* between "acts", "facts", "thoughts" and "deeds" and the *movement* that sustains them. Here the "living unison" (Geddes in Macdonald (ed.), 1992, 43) of place-work-folk is best understood as a *tensional relationship* mediated by its middle term. Without this mediation place and folk become "mere abstractions" (Ibid.), expendable to a capitalocentric worldview. And the real *work* of synergy—"of working together to solve problems and create opportunities" (Macdonald, 2020, 97)—will lack political bite. i.e. a standpoint (or outlook) from which to interpret and change the world.

10. For example, when Geddes collapses the tension between place-work-folk into a "simple chain, henceforward *unbroken*" [my italics] (Geddes in Macdonald (ed.), 1992, 33).

Hence *Future Fruit*'s commitment to the practice and metaphor of grafting: rather than elide the difference between nature and culture, it's the division itself, the *visible graft*, that keeps the relationship open; that allows for the "Re-education, Re-creation, and [...] Reconstruction [..] of Culture in its literal sense, of 'to cultivate'" (Geddes in ibid., 158). This matters for Geddes's understanding of the good life because the good life—which Geddes models in his theory of civics—is *always* "in the making"; open and revisable; never fixed (White in Welter, 2002, 49).

The importance of this distinction for *Future Fruit* can be seen in my earlier statement about the *polis*—a historically contingent practice that assumes a partition of the sensible: what is and isn't included; who can and can't speak. Whether that partition refers to the exclusion of slaves, women and children (as in the early Greek *polis*) or to the exclusion of agential subjects within a more-than-human world (as in neoliberal discussions of environmental sustainability), the difference has a common root. It's an example of structural violence; *an exclusionary principle that fails to recognise its own contingency.* Hence *Future Fruit*'s wager that a community orchard might fire up the wild bits of our collective imagination, the better to *resist* the standpoint of an *anti*-ecological worldview.

Yet despite *Future Fruit's* intention it's possible to read the story of *Future Fruit* critically, as a failure to graft intention and outcome. In short, when *Town is the Garden* closed in March 2020 institutional support for *Future Fruit* dried up and the artists and *Town is the Garden* staff had to reshuffle responsibilities for the orchard—handing on the vision and a small amount of funding to Huntly Climate Action.[11] While more could be said about this situation, detailed discussion would detract from the two-fold aim of this essay. But to ignore the discrepancy—the failed graft of intention and outcome—would undermine *Future Fruit's* hospitable critical wager. So, with that in mind I offer a brief shadow curatorial interjection. One that reads Geddes and Nuno Sacramento (the author of the Shadow Curator concept) as an example of Geddesian synthesis.

11. Since this essay was written the situation has moved on and Huntly Climate Action have in turn handed responsibility of the orchard to another, recently constituted, orchard group, Huntly Community Orchard, https://www.facebook.com/groups/2908085872645021/.

Interjection

The Shadow Curator concept can be summarised as "peaceful antagonism [...] through the use of dialogue and discussion, to challenge the proposals and actions of the curator in order to consolidate his/her [sic] methodology" (Sacramento and Zeiske, 2010, 16). It's to this task I now turn.[12]

Boldly put, I want to suggest that Deveron Projects' favoured methodology, "Town is the Venue", is founded on an *unsustainable* ambivalence—different, in principle, to the *productive* ambivalence of Claudia Zeiske's (Director of Deveron Projects 1995–21) wider interest in the concept of *unheimlich* (the

---

12. For faint hearted readers, or those unfamiliar with the Shadow Curator concept, it's worth reiterating that the following critique is part and parcel of Deveron Projects' methodology. It's directed towards Claudia Zeiske because Zeiske is (or was at the time of writing) the Director and curator of Deveron Projects, responsible for ongoing programming. That Zeiske welcomes hospitable criticality should be borne in mind throughout. Hence Zeiske's willingness to "loose ideas [...] free your thinking, watch from [a] different angle, see the obvious, forget the marketing" (Zeiske in Jacob and Zeiske (eds.), 2014, 18).

unhomely/uncanny). This ambivalence can be seen in Zeiske's decision not to support *Future Fruit* to its fruition. The reason for this decision was ostensibly pragmatic: Deveron Projects had other commitments. But here I want to suggest that Zeiske's decision reveals a deeper ambivalence regarding the usefulness, or not, of art—an ambivalence common to the artworld.[13] Specifically, whether Deveron Projects is in the business of offering "solutions" or generating "understanding" (Zeiske in Sacramento and Zeiske, 2010, 138–9). To parse these two terms as an either/or distinction weakens both possibilities and leaves Deveron Projects pray to an ever-changing outlook: a series of projects that "gaze" but don't "dwell". Here I borrow from Sacramento (in Jacob and Zeiske (eds.), 2014, 52) and I read Sacramento's distinction between gazing and dwelling as a shadow curatorial challenge for Deveron Projects—one that works with, not against, Deveron Projects' evolution-involution.

13. Here I have in mind Peter Osborne's description of the "systemic functionalization of autonomy (this new 'use' of art's 'uselessness')" and the way it integrates into "the logics of international politics and regional development" (Osborne, 2013, 21).

In short, I'm raising a hospitable critical question about Zeiske's *curatorial* ambivalence regarding the usefulness, or not, of art. And I'm proposing (in line with Geddes) that *Town is the Garden*—and its intended legacy, *Future Fruit*—might offer a more valuable (because ecological) methodology to that of "Town is the Venue". The difference can be summarised as follows: where "venue" implies the temporary, experimental use of a building (or in this case, a town), "garden" implies ongoing cultivation. Hence the following quote from Geddes can be read as a reflective challenge for Deveron Projects:

> growth seems slow: and people are all out for immediate results, like immediate votes or immediate money [or short-term residencies and projects]. A garden takes years and years to grow—ideas also take time to grow, and while a sower knows when his [sic] corn will ripen, the sowing of ideas is, as yet, a far less certain affair.[14]

How this relates to Sacramento's distinction

14. "Farewell lecture".

between gazing and dwelling can be developed as follows:

> We ought to create a world where everyone, independent of nationality, ethnicity, race, gender, financial situation, and level of dexterity, becomes a dweller. The capacity to dwell must become a commons. Our organisations and institutions—from schools to museums, from universities to arts organisation, from activist groups to civic associations, and so forth—must be mobilised towards the creation and sustainable maintenance of a commons of dwelling.
>
> The fact that everyone must be called forward to learn and practice dwelling, and then to be able to share this knowledge with others, will make it a commons. This entails an awareness of one's environment, followed by the capacity to act responsibly within it. We need to be enskilled to: (i) become aware and perceptive about our environment and (ii) organise our taskscape, i.e. the way to interact with our environment (Sacramento in Jacob and

Zeiske (eds.), 2014, 52).

While more could be said about this interjection—including the way Geddes's thinking is predicated on his formation as a gardener—here I offer this challenge as a methodological *support* for Zeiske's recent claim that Deveron Projects is now, after twenty-five years, taking the town's fate into its own hands.[15] This by working in collaboration with Huntly and District Development Trust to regenerate the Town Square—in part, by purchasing a building and launching Neep and Okra Kitchen. Suffice to say, for these initiatives to ripen into a Geddesian harvest—a synthesis of place-work-folk—the model of social and economic regeneration they perform would need to be rooted in long-term practices of ecological care (not just short-term projects or topic-led curation). And a good place to start (or continue) might be the maintenance, care and celebration of Huntly's community orchard.

Failing to forget

15. See Zeiske (2020) [video], https://www.ads.org.uk/pscf2020_deveronarts.

So, if this is the wager of *Future Fruit*, what role did Geddes play in the project? Specifically, what role did Geddes play in *Future Fruit*'s attempt to provide a set of social and ecological practices to cultivate evolutionary remembering?

The primary role Geddes played was as a *masque of learning*—a form of civic education through performance.[16] Here we took Geddes at his word and turned Geddes into performance art. In doing so we were assisted by Petra Pennington (Art and Community Worker for Deveron Projects) whose interpretation of our performance scores brought Geddes vividly to life. These performances affected a queer appropriation. Not Geddes the "man" or Geddes the "Indo-European mythologiser", but Geddes as a *mask* of learning; a creative *re*-performance open to *critical* appropriation.

To this end, *Future Fruit* appropriated Geddes's triadic understanding of place-work-folk, the orchard-related metaphors and analogies Geddes

16. Here I draw on Geddes's *The Masque of Learning and its Many Meanings* (1912) and Geddes's general use of masques and pageants to dramatise the history of civilisation. For a useful overview, see Broadman (1978, 234–40).

uses to describe this relationship and Geddes's wider use of thinking machines (of which the triad place-work-folk is one). These Geddesian readymades were explored through a variety of means: a film night, a reading group, a lunchtime talk, an MA site-visit, two maintenance and care workshops (one for pruning, one for grafting), community apple pressing, tree planting, silkscreen print workshops, and a penultimate event called, *Graft*—where the energy of *Future Fruit* was grafted through food, story and song onto the launch of Neep and Okra Kitchen. Yet rather than describe the arc of these events, I want to concentrate on a single event called *Aeons and Apple Trees*; a family-friendly engagement that took place during our August residency. In describing this event and the thinking that inspired it I hope to offer a *valley view* of *Future Fruit's* approach to socially engaged art and the way we rethought Huntly from a Geddesian perspective.[17]

17. In what follows I braid Geddes's Valley Section diagram—which begins high up in the mountains and then follows the course of a river down the mountains and through a plain toward its estuary at the coast—with Timothy Morton's Uncanny Valley *as* Spectral Plain—a plain (which in the case of

Aeons and Apple Trees

As the title suggests, *Aeons and Apple Trees* sought to link the orchard to a wider temporal context, a context Geddes would describe as "a drama in time".[18] With this provocation in mind we leapt from our conceptual Outlook Tower and landed in Huntly's community orchard.[19]

> *Future Fruit* is a flood plain) where the distinction between alive and not alive, sentient and non-sentient, and between conscious and unconscious is less certain. See Morton (2018, 180–183).
>
> 18. The full quote reads, "But a city is more than a place in space, it is a drama in time". For the wider context of this quotation, see The Oval Partnership (2020), https://www.ovalpartnership.com/en/article/item/The-Living-City-The-Rise-and-Fall-and-Rise-Again-of-Sir-Patrick-Geddes.
>
> 19. Geddes's Outlook Tower has been described as "a milestone in the history of urban design", see The Oval Partnership (2020). It was a real building in Edinburgh (still operating as the City's Camera Obscura) and an exemplary thinking machine. Geddes described the Outlook Tower as "[an] incipient Civic Observatory and Laboratory together—a type of institution needed [...] in every city with its effort towards correlation of thought and action, science and practice, sociology and morals, with its watchword and endeavour of 'Civic Survey for Civic Service'" (Geddes in Marshall Stalley

The image of leaping from a conceptual Outlook Tower and landing in an orchard is an apt description of what two artists might do when invited to reanimate a community orchard with Geddes in mind—to re-graft "understanding" and "solutions" in pursuit of a "useful" outcome. In the first instance we drew on Geddes's advise of "diagnosis before treatment" and undertook a process of engagement loosely analogous to Geddes's recommendations for a "regional survey" (see Geddes in Stalley, 1972, 239). For example, we researched Huntly's history—aided in part by Patrick W. Scott's *The History of Strathbogie* (2003). We spoke to Huntly citizens about contemporary politics—Brexit and climate change being live issues at the time. And we liaised with Huntly and District Development Trust to ensure that any subsequent proposals would complement Huntly's "Room to Thrive Strategy"—specifically the working document, "A Campus for Learning

(ed.), 1972, 239). More concretely the Outlook Tower functioned as an experiential research lab for understanding Edinburgh's urban evolution, whilst arguing for small-scale incremental development and change rather than wholesale demolition and redevelopment.

and Play".[20] Throughout this process we had in mind Philip Boardman's (1978) broad brushstroke description of the raison d'être of a regional survey and Geddes's direct advice that one needs to be "in love and at home with [one's] subject" (Geddes in Stephen (ed.), 2007, 43).

> Every region [...] has its heritage of good and its burden of evil. Every inhabitant should strive to know what his [sic] region contains, not only its wealth of natural resources, scenic beauty and heritage of culture but the opposite picture as well: the evils of ugliness, poverty, crime and injustice. The citizen must first study all these things with the utmost realism, then seek to preserve the good and abate the evil with the utmost idealism (Boardman, 1978, 141).

This is another way of saying that every place (and orchard) has its positive and negative attributes. That one should cultivate the positive

---

20. See Ice Cream Architecture (2019), http://www. huntly.town/campus/about/.

and minimise the negative. And this assumes the sort of political negotiations I mentioned above. The orchard becomes a *polis*. It provides a forum for debating and enacting *particular* models of human and more-than-human flourishing; of turning thought into action by re-grafting place-work-folk.

In the case of *Future Fruit*, we argued *against* the suggestion of extending the orchard through a process of rewilding—when rewilding, in this case, suggested planting more fruit trees without thought for their maintenance and care. We also argued *against* the orchard receiving funding from Tesco—when Tesco (and other supermarkets) use their "charitable" giving to greenwash their anti-ecological practices.[21] Instead, we argued *for* a "multi-species commons"—where humans and the more-than-human world would be entangled through acts of inter-species giving and receiving.[22]

21. For a broader discussion of this issue, see Small (2013, 51–63). Small draws on Geddes's thinking to underpin his proposal for a local food revolution, see Small (89–106).
22. Here we drew on two sources: Jennifer Marshman (2019), https://www.academia.edu/39155344/ Communing_with_bees_A_whole_of_community_ approach_to_address_crisis_in_the_Anthropocene; and Friday and Kerr in Sholette and Bass (2018),

ARBOR SÆCULORUM

P G

And we argued *for* social practices of ecological remembering where the orchard might become a living example of Geddes's *Arbor Saeculorum* (tree of the generations) and a forum for firing up the wild bits of our collective imagination by reimagining the *polis* through place-work-folk.

https://www.academia.edu/36902449/Designing_a_Multi_Species_Commons_A_Lesson_Plan_SPURSEmmons_A_Lesson_Plan_SPURSE).

Enough!

But enough of what we did and didnt argue for, what did we actually do? To answer this question, I focus on the specific forms of social and ecological remembering introduced in the context of *Aeons and Apple Trees*.

For *Aeons and Apple Trees* we took Geddes' concept of the Outlook Tower and collapsed it into a horizontal thinking machine. We did this by choreographing three walks and a run—the former to complement Deveron Projects' Walking Institute programme. The walks were a Cosmic Walk (otherwise known as a Deep Time Walk), a Biodiversity Walk and a Labyrinth Walk. The Cosmic Walk travelled from the past to the present. The Biodiversity Walk explored the current biodiversity of the orchard and wider Meadows area. And the Labyrinth Walk offered an opportunity for individuals to envisage a renewed future for the orchard—including their own commitment to its maintenance and care. In choreographing these walks we hoped to stage a drama in time; to bring the past, present and future together in one orchard chord.

As for the run, this was less pinned down. It

involved a repeat circumnavigation of the orchard by Fi Thomson for the duration of the Cosmic Walk.[23] For the purpose of this essay all I need to say about the run is that it signified the life-force needed to "compose and sustain what is and will be" (Haraway, 2016, 42); a life-force we described as *tentacular*.[24]

Beginning with the Cosmic Walk, it was here that we introduced Geddes to Huntly. "Summoned", as we said on the day, "from the uncanny valley of his death to the valley view of a new performance!"[25] Here Geddes, with fine red

23. Fi offered her service as an "independent" runner for the day. But it was important for *Future Fruit* that Fi was a member of the original Networks of Wellbeing team responsible for planting part of the orchard. Thus, Fi's presence symbolised the coming together of past, present and future possibilities for the orchard.

24. Here I acknowledge a debt to Donna Haraway's use of the term "tentacular", described as a "noninnocent, risky, committed, 'becoming involved in one another's lives'" (Haraway, 2016, 71).

25. This summons assumed Haraway's (2016) description of "The Speakers for the Dead [who] seek and release the energies of the past, present and future Chthulucene [i.e. as 'an unfurling Gaia'] (168, 51) and Morton's (2018) description of an "Uncanny Valley" (braided with Geddes' Valley Section), as "a forbidden zone filled with uncanny

beard and time travel umbrella, introduced himself [sic] as a "son" of Ballatar (a town in Aberdeenshire) and explained why he was here in Huntly: "To share with you [a deep time] story and to warn you of what's in store!" After a winning introduction (scored by Pennington), Geddes invited us to join him on a cosmic tour of the orchard:

> This is a story, the story of the Cosmos. Mystery generates wonder and wonder generates awe. Today we take a glimpse at the beauty of our Cosmic Story [...]. It is the story of the universe, the story of Earth, the story of all species, the story of you and I. [...] So come with me as we walk the *Chord of Life*.[26]

beings that reside scandalously in the Excluded Middle [of Cartesian dualism and the 'clean difference' of humans and Nature]" (Morton, 181–2).

26. The text we created for Geddes's cosmic tour was a cut-up of various online resources and quotations. Specifically: Worship Words (n.d.), https://www.worshipwords. co.uk/the-cosmic-walk-sister-miriam-therese-mcgillis-usa; North Carolina Interfaith Power & Light (2014), https://www.ncipl.org/wp-content/uploads/2014/07/ CosmicWalkComprehensive.pdf; Richter (2015), https:// www.cosmosmagazine.com/palaeontology/big-five-extinctions; Barlow and Dowd (2002), http://www.

After that, Geddes was off. A whirl of facts and invited actions as we paused to consider key moments in the forming and transforming of space and time. Starting 13.7 billion years ago Geddes introduced us to "the Great Emergence" when the universe first flashed into existence. We then leapt, skipped and danced through the aeons as Geddes described the birth of galaxies, solar systems, rain, cells, photosynthesis, sexual procreation, sight, plants, forests, dinosaurs, humans, agriculture, religion, science, and so much more; all leading, by way of evolution-involution, to the present day. In doing so, Geddes also drew our attention to five previous mass extinctions, when the majority of life on earth was wiped out. A theme Geddes returned to as he brought us home to the present day, a time of wonder *and* mass extinction. Geddes concluded his tour as follows:

> [We live during a] time when as many as 150 species are destroyed each day. A time that many of us now call the

thegreatstory.org/timeline.html; Wikipedia (n.d.), https://www.en.wikipedia.org/wiki/Rhynie_chert; McFadyen (2015), https://www.mairimcfadyen.scot/blog/2015/8/2/Patrick-geddes.

Anthropocene. A time in which humans are the primary cause of untold earthly suffering, of cataclysmic climate change and ecological breakdown. [A time in] which *your* children, *our* children will likely pay the price.

What must we do? ... Rebel for life!

We must cease to think merely in terms of separated departments and faculties and must relate all that we have seen today to the living mind; the ecological mind. And above all, we must adopt the *outlook of the artist*. [We must] see through the eyes of the ecologist, the school striker, the peasant farmer, the parent who cares for their child, and the politician who finally speaks the truth. We must begin with a small seed of possibility and invest that seed in place, work and folk. [...]

We have walked the Chord of Life. Now let it sing!

Beyond the overwhelm of facts that Geddes

brought to our attention, it was Geddes's *wonder* that held our imagination—with participants nodding their way through the deep time journey, face-to-face with rosebay willowherb and fruit tree, anticipating the next cosmic turn, and looking inward to consider their own cosmic significance. The way the walk ended had a profound effect on me (as someone now standing at a distance and taking photographs). I was struck by the way the participants emerged from the narrow pathway and formed an unruly semicircle around Geddes. When Geddes spoke the words, "a small seed of possibility", he started handing out seeds to the participants. What struck me about this moment (partly intended but not anticipated in this way) was how many of the participants lifted their hands with outstretched, upward-facing, overlapping palms—like someone receiving communion bread. Whether conscious or otherwise, this gesture could not have been more powerful. Nor could the attentive silence that followed the final Chord of Life which Geddes wrung from his fellow travellers: a cosmic Om of "[s]tar-wonder, stone and spark wonder, life-wonder, folk-wonder"[27]

27. "Farewell lecture".

which the Cosmic Walk had set out to inspire.

In many ways the event could have ended then. After all, a journey through deep time offers much to reflect upon! But after a few minutes to recuperate—and given a choice of taking a break now or later—participants were then invited to join John Malster (a former council ranger, now advocate for native wild flower meadows) on a Biodiversity Walk. This walk was mostly unscripted.[28] It was programmed to draw attention to the biodiversity of the orchard and the wider Meadows area; to cultivate what Geddes would later, at a tree planting ceremony, describe as an appreciation for "sunset and sunrise, moon and stars, the wonders of the winds, clouds and rain, the beauty of woods[, orchards,] and fields".[29]

Malster started by drawing our attention to the ground beneath our feet, which drawing on Geddes we could call *a hidden outlook*. It was the soil, Malster said, that sustained all that we could

28. Although formally unscripted, Malster's talk was originally staged to supply source material for an intended graphic novel. Specifically, a drawing of Geddes referring to the demonstration garden used during his farewell lecture at University College Dundee, 1919.

29. "Farewell lecture".

see around us: the fruit and nut trees, the wild flowers, all other verdant life, and the creatures—including ourselves. Having caught our attention, Malster then changed tack and observed that the "wild" cornflowers we were standing next to were more problematic than their popularity suggested. In short, they were the result of industrial-agricultural land management methods that limited biodiversity and depleted the soil through the use of chemical sprays such as Glyphosate.

With this warning as backdrop Malster then introduced his colleague Helen Rowe (a current council ranger) and set about describing some of the positive biodiversity attributes of the orchard and wider Meadows area. First, we were invited to take a closer look at the moths caught in Malster and Rowe's no-harm night traps. This part of the walk was designed to engage younger participants but the adults were equally enchanted. And through the gentle handling of moths and their release back into the orchard, we got a more visceral sense of what it meant to experience the orchard as a multi-species commons.

Following our encounter with the moths, we turned our attention to the companion plants. First, we observed what was already growing in

44

abundance: rosebay willowherb, ragwort, vetch, cleavers etc. Then Malster asked us what else one might expect to be growing and why it wasn't growing here already. This opened up a conversation about native and foreign plants and the pros and cons of taking an open or closed approach to local biodiversity. We also discussed the merits of reintroducing cattle and other livestock to break up the soil and create the right conditions to sustain a native perennial meadow.

As one might expect, these discussions generated a great deal of interest and strayed into what a number of participants recognised as politically loaded territory—at least by analogy. Who owns the land? How do we manage it? What constitutes a native species? When is a foreign species welcome? How do you regenerate a landscape already colonised by dominant plants and industrial-agricultural processes?

These questions, coupled with our multi-species encounters, helped us consider what it might mean to care for the orchard as a multi-species commons. The primary challenges being: who owns the land, who decides the rules and who does the work?

More could be said about the Biodiversity Walk but I now want to turn to the Labyrinth Walk—

albeit briefly. The first thing to say is that Sarah and I constructed the labyrinth using drift wood deposited on the flood plain—gently shaking off the spiders and insects who'd made their homes in the wood deposits. Having gathered the wood, we then constructed the labyrinth at a location identified for planting by *Town is the Garden*. Beyond the possibility of planting more fruit and nut trees, we thought the location leant itself to the construction of an outdoor education space; a play space designed to function as a simplified Geddesian Outlook Tower. We imagined this Outlook Tower rising from an orchard design based on Geddes's The Notation of Life diagram— thus a formal orchard augmented by Geddes's conceptual schema. As with Geddes's Outlook Tower, one would survey the wider region from a viewing platform before descending through the tower to learn more about Huntly's history and present circumstance.

Mindful of this idea—but considering our limited budget—we laid out the labyrinth as a nod to future possibilities, whilst also recognising the power of labyrinths to create their *own* dreamwork. An A-frame chalk board was also positioned adjacent to the labyrinth, on which we'd written:

47

A labyrinth is an ancient symbol that relates to wholeness. It represents a journey to our own centre and back again—out into the world. Labyrinths have long been used as meditation and prayer tools. Today we're asking everyone who walks the labyrinth to ask themselves the question, how might this space become a place of transformation for Huntly?

Clearly this question was open-ended. And *Future Fruit* had no desire to tie the future down. Instead, we took seriously Geddes's emphasis on the *inner* outlook of our walkers, trusting them to connect their "thoughts [and] ('dreams')" with the "acts" and "facts" of the morning's walks and other considerations. In doing so we hoped to strike a "Chord of Expression in Effective Life" and encourage movement into the fourth quadrant of Geddes's The Notation of Life diagram; the quadrant marked "deeds". To this end we hoped that walking the labyrinth might contribute to an "achieved Synergy"; a re-grafting of place-work-folk through a renewed commitment to the community orchard.

48

A beginning

Of course, the above walks and run were part of a wider engagement. An engagement cut short, as it happens. But I hope this brief description adds something to my earlier discussion of the Geddesian underpinning and hospitable critical wager of *Future Fruit*: that the maintenance, care and celebration of a community orchard might have the capacity to fire up the wild bits of our imagination, to help rethink the good life in relation to the more-than-human world and to mitigate—where possible—the worst affects of the climate and ecological crisis through the re-grafting of place-work-folk.

It's with this wager in mind that Sarah and I now don a final Geddesian mask and raise our Huntly wassail cup:

> Of this first [iteration] it is a main success to have demonstrated its own incompleteness: our present documentation is but a beginning (Geddes in Stalley (ed.), 1972, 267).

(Dedicated to the citizens of Huntly, to everyone

49

we worked with at Deveron Projects and *Town is the Garden*, to the current MCs of Huntly's community orchard, and to the orchard itself, with thanks.)

References

Barlow, Connie., and Dowd, Michael. "Epic of Evolution Timeline". *The Great Story* (2002). Accessed online. http://www.thegreatstory.org/timeline.html

Baxter, Jonathan., and Gittins, Sarah. *DUO (Dundee Urban Orchard)* (2013–17). https://www.dundeeurbanorchard.net

Bennett, Jane. *Vibrant Matter: A Political Ecology of Things* (Durham: Duke University Press, 2010).

Bollier, David. *Think Like a Commoner: A Short Introduction to the Life of the Commons* (Gabriola Island: New Society Publishers, 2014).

Broadman, Philip. *The Worlds of Patrick Geddes: Biologist, Town Planner, Re-educator, Peace-warrior* (London: Routledge, 1978).

Friday, Matthew., and Kerr, Iain. "Designing a Multi-Species Commons: A Lesson Plan". In Gregory Sholette, Chloë Bass, Social Practice Queens (eds.). *Art as Social Action: An Introduction to the Principles and Practices of Teaching Social Practice Art* (Allworth Press, 2018). Accessed online. https://www.academia.edu/36902449/ Designing_a_Multi_Species_Commons_A_ Lesson_Plan_SPURSE

Geddes, Patrick. *The Masque of Learning and its Many Meanings* (Edinburgh: Patrick Geddes and Colleagues, 1912).

——*Cities in Evolution: An Introduction to the Town Planning Movement and to the Study of Civics* (London: Williams and Norgate, 1915).

——"Patrick Geddes's farewell lecture to his Dundee students, 1919". Murdo Macdonald (ed.) (n.d.). Accessed online. https://www. murdomacdonald.wordpress.com/patrick-geddes-farewell-lecture-to-his-dundee-students-1919

Haraway, Donna J. *Staying with the Trouble: Making Kin in the Chthulucene* (Durham: Duke University Press, 2016).

Ice Cream Architecture. "Campus for Learning and Play". Huntly and District Development

Trust (2019). Accessed online. http://www.huntly.town/campus/about/

Jacob, Mary Jane., and Zeiske, Claudia (eds.). *Fernweh: A Travelling Curator's Project* (Berlin: JOVIS Verlag GmbH, 2014).

King, Angela., and Clifford, Sue. *Community Orchards: Handbook* (Shaftesbury: Common Ground, 2008).

Kropotkin, Peter. *Mutual Aid: A Factor of Evolution*, Mineola (New York: Dover Publications, [1902]2006).

Mabey, Richard. *Nature Cure* (London: Pimlico, 2006).

Macdonald, Murdo (ed.). *Patrick Geddes: Ecologist, Educator, Visual Thinker* (Edinburgh: Edinburgh Review 22, 1992).

———*Patrick Geddes's Intellectual Origins*. (Edinburgh: Edinburgh University Press, 2020).

Marshman, Jennifer. "Communing with bees: A

whole-of-community approach to address crisis in the Anthropocene". *Journal of Agriculture, Food Systems, and Community Development* (2019). Accessed online. https://www.academia.edu/39155344/Communing_with_bees_A_whole_of_community_approach_to_address_crisis_in_the_Anthropocene

McFadyen, Mairi. "The Cultural-Ecological Imagination of Patrick Geddes (1854–1932)". *Northlight* (2015). Accessed online. https://www.mairimcfadyen.scot/blog/2015/8/2/patrick-geddes?rq=patrick%20geddes

Morton, Timothy. *Being Ecological* (London: Pelican, 2018).

North Carolina Interfaith Power & Light. "Cosmic Walk" (2014). Accessed online. https://www.ncipl.org/wp-content/uploads/2014/07/CosmicWalkComprehensive.pdf

Osborne, Peter. *Anywhere or Not at All: Philosophy of Contemporary Art* (London: Verso, 2013).

The Oval Partnership. "The Living City—The Rise and Fall, and Rise Again of Sir Patrick Geddes" (2020). Accessed online. https://www.ovalpartnership.com/en/article/item/The-Living-City-The-Rise-and-Fall-and-Rise-Again-of-Sir-Patrick-Geddes

Puig de la Bellacasa, María. *Matters of Care: Speculative Ethics in More than Human Worlds* (Minneapolis: University of Minnesota Press, 2017).

Rancière, Jacques. *The Politics of Aesthetics: The Distribution of the Sensible* (London: Continuum, 2004).

Richter, Viviane. "The big five mass extinctions". *Cosmos Magazine* (2015). Accessed online. https://www.cosmosmagazine.com/palaeontology/big-five-extinctions

Sacramento, Nuno., and Zeiske, Claudia. *ARTocracy: Art, Informal Space, and Social Consequence: A Curatorial Handbook in Collaborative Practice* (Berlin: JOVIS Verlag GmbH, 2010).

Santner, Eric L. *On the Psychotheology of Everyday Life: Reflections on Freud and Rozensweig* (Chicago: The University of Chicago Press, 2001).

Scott, Patrick W. *The History of Strathbogie* (Tiverton: XL Publishing Services, revised edition, 2003).

Seed, John (et al.), illustrations by Pugh, Dailan. *Thinking Like a Mountain: Towards a Council of All Beings* (Gabriola Island: New Catalyst Books, 2007).

Small, Mike. *Scotland's Local Food Revolution* (Glendaruel: Argyll Publishing, 2013).

Stalley, Marshall (ed.). *Patrick Geddes: Spokesman for Man and the Environment* (New Jersey: Rutgers University Press, 1972).

Stephen, Walter (ed.). *A Vigorous Institution: The Living Legacy of Patrick Geddes* (Edinburgh: Lauth Press, 2007).

Welter, Volker M. *Biopolis: Patrick Geddes and the City of Life* (Cambridge, Massachusett: The MIT

Press, 2002).

Wikipedia. "Rhynie Chert" (n.d.). Accessed online. https://www.en.wikipedia.org/wiki/Rhynie_chert

Worship Words. "Cosmic Walk, an interactive ritual" (n.d.). Accessed online. https://www.worshipwords.co.uk/the-cosmic-walk-sister-miriam-therese-mcgillis-usa

Zeiske, Claudia (ed.). *PRAKTIKA: Huntly, Aberdeenshire: Socially engaged art practice* (Deveron Arts, 2008).

——"Deveron Projects" [video]. *Architecture and Design Scotland* (2020). Accessed online. https://www.ads.org.uk/pscf2020_deveronarts/

60

Huntly Orchard tea recipe
Joss Allen

62

(Or rosebay willowherb tea)

The orchard in Huntly was almost completely overgrown with rosebay willowherb (Chamerion angustifolium) when we began to work with it. What to do about the willowherb was an ongoing debate: it had enveloped the orchard in a protective *weedy* layer for many years but it had also kept it partially hidden and inaccessible.

In our research into what we might do with the willowherb, we came across a recipe for turning it into tea. This became a yearly ritual for us, around August or September, we would harvest a crop of rosebay willow leaves and flowers to ferment and the dry into tea.

According to a variety of sources, rosebay willowherb tea was once more popular to drink than black tea in the UK, and was even imported from Russia. I think the tea is similar to green tea but with more grassy, floral notes. It's very refreshing, caffeine free and believed to promote relaxation, improve mood and concentration, and aid digestion. Perfect for drinking at afternoon meetings.

Rosebay willowherb is such a fascinating plant, and to learn more about it we recommend seeking out Richard Mabey's *Weeds* (2010), which has a whole chapter dedicated to it.

Recipe

Collect leaves and flowers (keep them separate for now) on a dry, sunny day in summer (they could still be picked in September in Huntly).

Set aside the flowers for later (if picked). Scrunch up the leaves into little balls and allow to ferment for a few days, either in a plastic bag, bucket or large kilner jar. You can adjust the fermentation period to suit your particular taste, or skip entirely. Check it daily as over fermentation will lead to mould developing as it starts to decompose.

Spread out the leaves and flowers onto trays, a clean table or window sill, and leave to dry. This could take a couple of days depending on where you leave them. You can also use a dehydrator if you have one, or an oven on very low.

Once dried pack into dry containers which you have secure lids for. The tea will last at least about a year, if kept dry and out of sunlight. Use as you would other dried herbs for tea making.

References

Eat Weeds. "Rosebay Willowherb – A Foraging Guide to Its Food, Medicine and Other Uses" (n.d.). https://www.eatweeds.co.uk/rosebay-willowherb-epilobium-angustifolium.

Mabey, Richard. *Weeds* (London: Profile Books, 2010.

Joss Allen can be found at the edges of the garden, amongst the weeds and compost heaps. He is an artworker and gardener exploring how creative practices can shape earthy politics, community economies and ecological ways of being in playful, radical, responsive and meaningful ways.

Jonathan Baxter and Sarah Gittins braid individual art practices with a collaborative commitment to addressing the climate and ecological crisis.

Since 2009 Jonathan has combined the roles of artist, curator and peer-educator to deliver a series of participatory art projects and peer-learning programmes. These include Dundee Artists in Residence *(2009-12),* Dundee Urban Orchard *(2013-17),* On Site Projects, *Dundee (2013-18),* Arts and Communities Programme, *Aberdeen (2016-17),* Murmur: Artists Reflect on Climate Change, *Ullapool (2017), and* Future Fruit, *Huntly (2019-20). Since 2012 Jonathan has worked under the auspices of A+E, a conceptual framework that braids the terms accident and emergency, art and ecology, art and education. Current projects include an embedded artist residency at St Mary's Episcopal Cathedral, Edinburgh (2020-2030) and a*

Craigmillar and Communities Walking Residency *with Art Walk Projects, Edinburgh (2021-ongoing). He supports various aspects of Extinction Rebellion's arts coordination and has a research interest in the philosophy of Gillian Rose.*

Sarah Gittins is a visual artist working across a variety of media, with a particular focus on drawing and printmaking. Her work explores issues of social and ecological justice, with a focus on climate change, land use and food sustainability. Sarah's images create a space where the activities of everyday life encounter incidents of global environmental concern, bringing those issues which are often pushed to the edges of consciousness into the here and now of personal awareness. Sarah is interested in the capacity of image-making to enable engagement, conversation and action for change. With this in mind, recent years have seen more performative approaches emerge within Sarah's solo work and in collaboration with Jonathan Baxter. Sarah is also a passionate art educator, currently leading the Figure Course at Leith School of Art and developing a programme of plant-based drawing adventures with A+E.

Town is the Garden

A community food growing project, *of sorts*.

For three years the Town is the Garden team could be found at the margins of the garden. Amongst the weeds and compost heaps, they explored what it might mean to *think with* the garden. Through crafting gardens, vegetable plots and orchards they attempted to rethink how a community might feed itself as it faces up to the global climate and ecological emergency. Through the processes of learning and sharing skills in relation to growing food, from planting seeds to preserving the harvest, they asked how we might also begin to pay better attention to the entanglement of human and more-than-human worlds. They asked how might the garden be a site of both resistance and resilience? A place for *thinking* and *doing* ecology, otherwise.

This is *Orchard* in a collection of seven chapbooks by the *Town is the Garden* that attempt to capture some of the diverse ways of thinking, doing and knowing the project explored with some of the people they explored them with. It includes contributions from Eleanor Brown and Alexandra Falter (*Plants*), Jonathan Baxter & Sarah Gittins (*Orchard*), Joe Crowdy (*Garden*), Dawn Finch

(*Seeds*), Maria Puig de la Bellacasa (*Compost*), and Joss Allen, Caroline Gatt and Elisabetta Rattalino (*Story*). With cover illustrations by Jamie Johnson.

The Town is the Garden team included: Joss Allen (2017–20), Rhian Davies (2019–20), Caroline Gatt (2018–20), Camille Sineau (2017–18), and Lindy Young (2017–19).

https://www.deveron-projects.com/town-garden

The *Town is the Garden* team would like to thank everyone who contributed to these chapbooks and Footprint Workers Cooperative for their exceptional printing skills.

A massive thank you to everyone at Deveron Projects, staff, board and interns (too many to name), especially Petra Pennington, Robyn Wolsey and Claudia Zeiske—for their support and guidance—and the Neep & Okra Kitchen team—with whom we latterly shared space and ideas with. To Alex Severn, our wonderful intern, on a student placement from the University of Aberdeen. To our generous funders Aberdeenshire Council, Action Earth, Climate Challenge Fund, Community Growing Fund, Creative Scotland, Finnis Scott Foundation, Groundwork, and Grow Wild. Many thanks to the Aberdeenshire Environmental Fo-

rum for awarding the Green Butterfly Award to Huntly Town, partly in recognition of the work of the *Town is the Garden* project. The award gave the team great encouragement.

We would like to thank everyone who took part in the *Town is the Garden* project, for their generosity, patience and support. In particular those who contributed to the programme: Matt Aitkenhead, Andy Smith, Charlie Ashton, Grace Banks, Rosa Bevan and James Reid, John Bolland, Stephen Brandes, Alan Carter, Karen Collins, Doug Cookson, Uist Corrigan, Bob Donald, David Easton and Jane Lockyer, Petra/Patrick Geddes, Katrina Flad, Marguerite Fleming, Vicky Flood, David Foubister, Cristina Grasseni, Charlie Hanks, Margaret and Andrew Lear, Leslie Mabon, John Malster, Ann Miller, Miranda Montgomery, Bryan Morrison, Joshua Msika, Lorna Patterson, Chris Pepper, Annabel Pinker, Ian Scott, Pat Scott, Christine Steiner, Emma Stewart, Katie Stewart, Andrew Tassell, Leanne Townsend, Nikki and James Yoxall, David Watts, the Grow it, Cook it, Eat it team at BBC Radio Scotland, and everyone at the Scottish Sculpture Workshop.

And finally to Yvonne Billimore, Richard Muscat and Mariuccia Muscat, for all kinds of care, encouragement, sharp-eyes and support throughout.

Town is the Garden Chapbooks: Orchard
Published by Deveron Projects and Intellect in 2021

Edited by Joss Allen and Caroline Gatt
Layout by Joss Allen
Cover illustrations by Jamie Johnson
Printed and bound by Footprint Workers Cooperative, Leeds

Typeface: Adobe Casion Pro / Garamond Pro
Paper: Context Natural / Evercopy Plus

ISBN 978-1-907115-37-0

Deveron Projects is a company limited by guarantee,
registered in Scotland No. SC391020 and a registered
Scottish Charity No. SC024261

Town is the Garden Chapbooks
Deveron Projects and Intellect